DANIEL BURNAP, EAST WINDSOR

MADE C. 1785

OWNED BY JAMES H. NAYLOR, HARTFORD

CONNECTICUT CLOCKMAKERS OF THE EIGHTEENTH CENTURY

PENROSE R. HOOPES

SECOND EDITION
with 60 illustrations
and a supplementary article,
"Some Minor Connecticut Clockmakers"

DOVER PUBLICATIONS, INC.
NEW YORK

Published in Canada by General Publishing Company, Ltd., 30 Lesmill Road, Don Mills, Toronto, Ontario.

Published in the United Kingdom by Constable and Company, Ltd., 10 Orange Street, London WC 2.

This Dover edition, first published in 1974, is an unabridged republication of the work originally published in 1930 by Dodd, Mead and Company, New York, and Edwin Valentine Mitchell, Hartford, to which has been added as an Appendix an article by Penrose R. Hoopes, "Some Minor Connecticut Clockmakers," that originally appeared in *The Magazine ANTIQUES*, Vol. 28, No. 3, Sept. 1935, pp. 104-105 (reproduced by courtesy of *The Magazine ANTIQUES*).

International Standard Book Number: 0-486-22922-X
Library of Congress Catalog Card Number: 72-93610

Manufactured in the United States of America
Dover Publications, Inc.
180 Varick Street
New York, N.Y. 10014

FOR

BETH BURRITT HOOPES

FOREWORD

THESE notes have been compiled almost wholly from the original records. When it has seemed necessary to express matters of opinion, or where inference or tradition is involved, the context will indicate the fact. No illusions are entertained as to the probable completeness or freedom from errors of the work.

I desire to express my appreciation for many courtesies and suggestions received from Mr. Henry W. Erving, Mr. George D. Seymour, Mr. William H. Putnam, Mr. Albert C. Bates and Mr. William Hubbard during the preparation of the manuscript. The staffs of The Connecticut Historical Society, Connecticut State Library, American Antiquarian Society, Yale University Library, New Haven Colony Historical Society and The Otis Library have been unfailingly helpful in making available the collections of these institutions. Special acknowledgement is tendered to Mr. William H. Putnam for the photographs used to illustrate the work, and to the owners of the clocks for permission to reproduce them herein.

P. R. H.

CONTENTS

Part One

CLOCKMAKING IN EIGHTEENTH CENTURY CONNECTICUT

Part Two

CLOCKMAKERS OF EIGHTEENTH CENTURY CONNECTICUT

PART ONE

CLOCKMAKING

IN

EIGHTEENTH CENTURY CONNECTICUT

CHAPTER I: THE PIONEERS

OF THE numberless arts and crafts practiced in pioneer America during the seventeenth and eighteenth centuries, none is of greater interest or significance than the work of the early clockmakers. The men of this craft established the first precision mechanical industry practiced on the American continent. They were the pioneer machinists, and the tiny shops in which they worked were the earliest machine shops furnished with metal turning lathes, gear cutting machines, wire drawing and screw cutting equipment, foundry and forge shop tools. Their work was of the most scientific, accurate and complex nature, their product was the most intricate known to the age in which they lived, and their influence upon the spread of sound technical skill was of incalculable value to the colonies.

The early clockmakers, like all of the pioneer craftsmen, were far from being narrow specialists. The making of a clock called for the exercise of the arts of the foundryman, blacksmith, engraver, pattern-maker, cabinet-maker and machinist. The clockmakers were therefore in the fortunate position of all around mechanics, perfectly capable of undertaking the construction of any small- or medium-sized metal product for which a demand might arise. They were able, in the long periods between the making of occasional clocks, to do a vast amount of other work, not only in such fields as clock and watch repairing, in which of course they excelled, but in the making of surveyor's and mariner's instruments, scales, mechanical jacks, bells, buttons, buckles, pumps, pewter-ware, tools, reeds and cards for textile processing, silver-ware, weathercocks, fire engines, printing presses, and, in one instance at least, a mechanical odometer to measure the distance passed over by a cart.

In spite of his versatility however, the colonial clockmaker was a full-fledged maker of complete clock movements. He forged, turned and cut the pinions; cast the wheels and plates from scrap brass purchased from his fellow townsmen; hammered, filed and polished the plates; laid out, drilled and broached the pivot holes; turned and cut the teeth in the wheels; hammered and engraved the dial; filed out the hands; and fitted and assembled the parts into the complete mechanism. In some instances he also made the clock case, although many of the early cases were the product of joiners or cabinet-makers whose chief business was the making of household furniture, men who were in no way directly associated with the clockmakers and who were totally unfamiliar with clock mechanisms.

The shops of the first American clockmakers differed in no way from those of the European craftsmen of the same period. In London, in Paris, or in Boston, the clockmaker in the year 1700 was an individual worker assisted only by his apprentice boy, employing but a few simple tools and carrying on a custom business in a room perhaps as large as ten feet square. No factories were in existence at that time, there were no specialists to furnish clock parts, and probably no stores other than the clockmakers' own establishments in which complete clocks could be purchased. The making of a clock presented no greater difficulties in America than in Europe, the methods and tools employed were identical, and the training and experience of the craftsmen were precisely the same.

The earliest American clockmakers were residents of Boston, and the first town clocks as well as some of the earliest privately owned clocks were to be found in that community. As early as 1668 Richard Taylor had charge of the Boston town clock. In 1670 he was replaced by Thomas Matson, Senior, a "gunsmith" who was employed "to looke after the towne clocke and keepe it in good repair . . . & to have 10s for his paines about it." From 1673 to some time after 1680 Giles Dyer was employed to "keepe the Clocke." He was paid five pounds in 1680 for "settinge up ye clocke at ye North Meeting House" and was employed to take care of this new clock as well as the old town clock. In 1684 the care of the "clocke at ye North end of the Towne" was entrusted to William Sumner, termed a "blacksmith," and in 1689 it was decreed that "Robert Williams shall carfullie looke after and keepe the Towne Clocke in the old Meeting House." Richard Taylor died in 1673, Thomas Matson in 1677 and Giles Dyer in 1713. William Sumner, "blacksmith," was born in Boston in 1656 and removed in 1687 to Middletown, Connecticut, where he died in 1703.

It is possible but by no means certain that some of these early keepers of the town clocks were actual clockmakers. During the eighteenth century, work of this character was often assigned to the leading clockmaker of the town where the clock was situated, and there is no reason to think that the custom may not have been followed from the very first. Whether the work which Giles Dyer did in 1680 in "settinge up ye clocke" was the construction of that clock or merely its installation and regulation, is unknown. Certainly, however, these men were repairers of clocks and were called upon to keep the few domestic clocks of seventeenth century Boston in running order. That William Sumner continued to repair an occasional lantern clock after his removal to Connecticut in 1687 is probable, but no evidence has been found to suggest that he actually constructed clocks while living in Middletown.

In 1683, William Davis, a clockmaker, arrived in Boston, and in 1687 the tax lists mentioned David Johnson, watchmaker. After the foundation of the first newspaper in Boston in 1704, there were detailed references to James Batterson in 1707, Isaac Webb in 1708, James Brand in 1711, Joseph Essex in 1712, William Claggett, Jr., in 1715, and others, all English clockmakers who were equipped and trained to carry through the complete construction of domestic clocks.

In both New York and Philadelphia the trade was well established before 1700. Everardus Bogardus is mentioned as a New York clockmaker and silversmith in 1698, and in the same year Gabriel Thomas wrote in his account of Pennsylvania that clock- and watch-makers were regularly working at their trades in Philadelphia prior to that date.

No centers of population comparable in size or wealth with Boston, New York or Philadelphia were to be found in Connecticut during the early eighteenth century, and it was therefore not until about the year 1712 that evidence appears of the existence of a clockmaker's shop in that colony. It was at about that date that Ebenezer Parmele commenced business in Guilford. He was born in Guilford in 1690, the son of a carpenter and cabinet-maker. Where he learned the trade of clockmaking is unknown, but it is not unlikely that he may have been sent to New York to work in the shop of one of the earliest Dutch craftsmen, perhaps as an apprentice to Bogardus the clockmaker and silversmith. Parmele was not only a clockmaker familiar with both brass and wooden clocks, but also a boatbuilder, chairmaker, a worker in wood and metals, and a trader. That he made any substantial number of clocks is unlikely, but he was nevertheless apparently the father of clockmaking in Connecticut. He was a man of prominence in his community, a skillful mechanic, and the maker of the first tower clock erected in the colony.

Apparently one of the first things that Ebenezer Parmele did after establishing himself in Guilford was to employ an apprentice. Throughout the craftsman period an apprentice was as much a part of the clockmaker's establishment as his tools or his shop.

The apprentice was a boy of from twelve to fourteen years of age who was bound by his parents to the clockmaker, the latter furnishing the lad with food, clothing and a place to sleep, and instructing him in the trade in return for his services. These services were at first in running errands, making up the forge fire, cleaning the shop and acting as a servant for the clockmaker. As the boy gradually picked up a knowledge of the elements of mechanical work he took his place at the forge or bench and assisted with the simpler parts of the productive work. Eventually he became sufficiently skilled to handle any of the work of the shop, and as a final proof of this skill he was usually required to construct a complete clock. He then received a certificate from his master, and taking the kit of tools which he had made during his apprenticeship, he moved to a neighboring town and opened a shop of his own. If the master clockmaker had a sufficient quantity and variety of work, more than one apprentice might be employed, and apparently this condition arose in Parmele's shop, for about 1714 he began to train two boys, Macock Ward who was born in 1702 in Wallingford, and his own nephew Abel Parmele who was born in Guilford in 1703.

Macock Ward was working on his own account as a clockmaker in Wallingford by 1724 and continued in the trade until his death in 1783. He was an unusually versatile mechanic, a clockmaker, tinker, joiner and buttonmaker, and was the most active and prominent politician in Wallingford prior to the Revolutionary War. He made tower clocks and both brass and wooden tall clocks, but unlike most of the later clockmakers, he constructed the cases for many of the clocks which he built. A majority of the eighteenth century Connecticut clocks were sold by their makers without cases, each purchaser contracting directly with a local cabinet-maker for a case to suit his taste and means. The term "clock" was applied to the mechanical unit made up of the movement proper, the dial, hands, pendulum and weights, while the case was invariably looked upon as a distinct item. That Ward was able to furnish both clock and case indicates that his early training was unusually thorough, and implies that Ebenezer Parmele himself also made the cases in which his clocks were housed.

Abel Parmele, Ebenezer's second apprentice, was, in addition to being a clockmaker, the first bell founder in Connecticut. As early as 1736 he petitioned the Assembly for a monopoly on the casting of large bells, a petition which was however not granted. Throughout the eighteenth century a number of the Connecticut clockmakers engaged in casting church bells. In 1738 John Whitear of Fairfield was in the business and was succeeded in 1762 by his son of the same name. The latter carried on the work until his death in 1773 when Isaac Doolittle of New Haven took up the business and continued it until the time of his death in 1800. In 1788 Enos Doolittle began casting bells in Hartford, and at about the same time Benjamin Hanks erected a bell foundry in Litchfield. All of these men were well known clockmakers, and all no doubt traced their knowledge of bell making directly or indirectly to Abel Parmele.

Seth Youngs, perhaps another apprentice to Ebenezer Parmele, was born in Southold, Long Island, in 1711, and after serving his apprenticeship, removed in 1735 to Hartford and later to Windsor. Not a great deal is known of his work as a clockmaker although at least one of his clocks is still in existence. He is the only one of the early craftsmen who is definitely known to have made hour glasses. It is probable that one of his first apprentices was Benjamin Cheney of East Hartford.

From Benjamin Cheney stemmed the East Hartford group of clockmakers known particularly for the making of wooden clocks with fine engraved and silvered brass dials. Benjamin Willard, the first of the noted Massachusetts family of clockmakers, received his initiation into the art in Cheney's shop, where John Fitch, the inventor of the steamboat, also served a partial apprenticeship.

Isaac Doolittle, born in Wallingford in 1721, was the most successful of Macock Ward's apprentices. Doolittle settled in New Haven prior to 1743 and for over fifty years was one of the outstanding mechanics of the colony. He made clocks, instruments, and small brass wares, cast church bells, operated one of the leading powder mills during the Revolution, built printing presses, and trained a number of apprentices. His nephew and apprentice Enos Doolittle settled in Hartford in 1772 and served that town for thirty years as a clockmaker, brass founder, instrument maker and bell founder. Among the New Haven clockmakers who probably owed their training to Isaac Doolittle mention might be made of Hezekiah Hotchkiss, Nathan Howell, Simeon Jocelin and Isaac Doolittle, Jr. Of these men, all of whom were born in New Haven, the most significant as a craftsman was perhaps Jocelin.

Simeon Jocelin was making clocks and repairing watches in New Haven as early as 1768 and continued in the business until his death in 1823. He was a man of varied interests, a talented mathematician, but best known for his work as a music publisher, an enterprise in which he was associated with the engraver, Amos Doolittle. He was one of the most scientific clockmakers and his shop was one of the most completely equipped of any of the Connecticut craftsmen, but his clocks, of which he undoubtedly made a substantial number, are not often found today.

A few of the prerevolutionary Connecticut clockmakers were trained in Massachusetts, Rhode Island and New York. Ebenezer Balch, born in Boston in 1723, learned his trade in that town and moved to Hartford in 1744, going later to Wethersfield, where it is presumed that he instructed David Lowrey in the art. Samuel Rockwell, born in Middletown in 1722, worked as an apprentice and master clockmaker in Providence, but returned to Middletown prior to 1762. Joseph Clark, working as a clockmaker in New York in 1768, removed to Danbury about 1772. Joseph Carpenter of Norwich, John Avery of Preston, Isaac Reed of Stamford and

Peregrine White of Woodstock were all working in their respective towns prior to the Revolutionary War, but although they were all natives of Connecticut, very little is known of their early training or experience.

No European born clockmaker of importance settled within the limits of the colony until the year 1773, when Thomas Harland emigrated from England, opened a shop in Norwich, and became the chief exponent of the craft in that part of Connecticut. Harland occupied a unique position in the annals of Connecticut clockmaking. He was without question the most skillful maker of clocks and the most energetic business man in the trade. A man of superior education and training, he attracted to his shop an astonishing number of talented apprentices, and but for the fact that his methods were strictly those of the craftsman, he might almost be credited with having established the first clock factory in America. Tradition says that he had as many as ten or twelve apprentices working at once in his shop, and contemporary records show that in 1795 his equipment was valued at some $1500.00, an enormous figure for that day. He not only made many beautiful brass clocks together with their cases, but he was the first man in Connecticut to make complete watches. His apprentices settled throughout the eastern counties of Connecticut and introduced clockmaking into many of the smaller towns between the Connecticut River and the Massachusetts line.

By the opening of the Revolutionary War the trade was being actively carried on in Fairfield, Stratford, New Haven, Wallingford, Wethersfield, Hartford, Middletown, Norwich, Preston, New London, East Hartford, Windsor, Litchfield, Danbury, Stamford and Woodstock.

During the war and for some years after its close clockmaking languished, and many of the clockmakers turned temporarily to more profitable occupations. Muskets, cannon, gun locks, gunpowder, powder sieves, salt, watch crystals, brass castings and nails were some of the articles to which they devoted their energies during this unsettled period. With the return of more normal conditions came a renewed demand for clocks, but due either to the current degeneration of taste in both Europe and America, or to the prevailing poverty following the war, the quality of many of the clocks made from this time on grew poorer.

The last quarter of the eighteenth century witnessed a substantial growth in the number of clockmakers as well as in the output of clocks. In the vicinity of New Haven the older men, Doolittle, Merriman and Jocelin continued without much competition, but in eastern Connecticut, while Harland maintained his outstanding position, his apprentices established small clock shops in Ashford, Canterbury, East Windsor, New London, Lyme, Mansfield, Windham, Norwich and Hartford. Some of these apprentices became men of importance in the trade. Daniel Burnap of East Windsor achieved the greatest technical success, but also worthy of note were Benjamin Hanks of Litchfield and Mansfield, William Cleveland and Nathaniel Shipman of Norwich, and Ezra Dodge of New London. In the realm of cheap wooden tall clocks Gideon Roberts of Bristol, Eli Terry of Plymouth and James Harrison of Waterbury were active during the closing years of the century.

About the year 1785 many of the makers of brass clocks gave up the foundry part of the work and began to purchase the brass castings for plates, pillars and wheels, simply filing, turning and cutting the teeth in the parts and fitting them together. Dials and hands were also often purchased, as were the metal ornaments used on cases, and in some instances even completed pinions were procured from dealers in clockmakers' supplies. Some of this material was imported but much of it was made locally in the small brass foundries. It is probable that the Doolittle foundry in Hartford turned out many of the castings used by the Connecticut clockmakers at the end of the century.

The elimination of the foundry and forge work from the clockmaker's craft resulted eventually in turning the craftsman into an assembler and his shop into the forerunner of the present day jewelry store, where watches, gold and silverware could be purchased, and where the mechanical work was largely confined to repairing and engraving, with clockmaking reduced to putting the finishing touches upon purchased parts, assembling them and regulating the clock. By 1820 it is probable that even this simplified form of so-called clockmaking had ceased, and clocks were thereafter made only in factories by machinery.

A very marked tendency for the younger craftsman clockmakers in Connecticut to entirely abandon the trade appeared about the year 1800. Several factors were responsible for this condition. The apprenticeship system and an influx of European craftsmen had increased the number of trained men in the business out of all proportion to the population and to the size of the market for high-class clocks. The cheap wooden movement clock, which could be produced much more rapidly and inexpensively than the metal clock, was becoming the accepted article for the middle classes and was being turned out by such men as Gideon Roberts, Eli Terry, John Rich, Elisha Cheney, the Harrisons and others upon a scale undreamed of during the eighteenth century; while the wealthier classes probably tended more and more to purchase the higher priced and more elaborate imported clocks which had been favored by the aristocracy of Boston and Providence from the beginning of the century. Trained as the clockmakers of that day almost invariably were in watch repairing, silversmithing and engraving, it was but natural that they should turn to these pursuits, becoming jewelers, spoon-makers and retailers of watches, necklaces and rings. With the introduction of the wooden shelf clock about 1815, the death knell of the craftsmen had sounded. The disappearance of the craft was more sudden and complete in Connecticut than, for example, in either Massachusetts or Pennsylvania. The latter states never developed a factory industry, and their craftsmen continued to struggle along for many years before finally succumbing one by one to business enterprise, competition, and the rising flood of cheap trade clocks.

In Connecticut, therefore, the period prior to 1800 may be considered as the one of true craftsmanship; the years from 1800 to 1820 as a transition era during which the factories appeared; and from 1820 to the present day as a time of purely commercial factory production.

CHAPTER II: EARLY CLOCKS

THE making of domestic clocks for general use was commenced in Europe about the year 1600, but prior to that date the verge and crown-wheel escapement, the striking mechanism, the spring drive and the fuzee were well known in the art. About 1658 the short or "bob" pendulum was first applied to clocks. The long case or "grandfather" clock appeared between 1660 and 1670 and the long or "royal" pendulum was introduced about 1676, at which time clocks were first made to run for eight days and were fitted with the anchor escapement. By the time that clockmaking was introduced into America, shortly prior to 1700, the domestic clock had been developed to such a point that no substantial improvement has been made from that day to the present. In other branches of horology, notably in chronometers, astronomical clocks and pocket watches, great progress was yet to come, but the domestic clocks of 1700, both spring-driven bracket clocks and weight-driven tall clocks, had reached a point of perfection perhaps never subsequently surpassed, and indeed but rarely equaled.

The first clocks used in America were the small brass lantern clocks designed to hang upon the wall or to stand on a wall bracket. They were weight operated, controlled by a balance wheel and verge escapement, had but one hand, struck the hours, and were imported from England certainly before 1640. They were by no means common, although a few of the leading men of the times counted such clocks among their possessions. Toward the end of the seventeenth century the merits of the pendulum had become so well established that most of the lantern clocks were altered to allow the use of a pendulum in place of the original balance wheel. This work of conversion was a by no means insignificant part of the duties of the earliest colonial clockmakers, a fact clearly evidenced by the advertisements of the Boston craftsmen during the first decade of the eighteenth century. It was this early "turning old clocks into pendulums" which accounts for the present condition of the few surviving lantern clocks which were originally used in America.

A few of the lantern clocks were doubtless ultimately provided with wooden cases, thus becoming hooded clocks. An early instance of such a clock is probably represented in the inventory of Rev. John Norton of Boston, who in 1663 owned a "clock and case." This clock may, of course, have been a tall case one, but its early date makes such an hypothesis improbable.

That a very few lantern clocks may have actually been made in America is not impossible, although so far as is now known, no domestic example has survived.

Perhaps the earliest record of the existence of a clock in Connecticut occurs in the will of Henry Packs, dated September 4, 1640. Packs bequeathed his clock to the church in Hartford. It was a small brass lantern clock of the domestic type, and not a public or tower clock. It is not certain that this clock was actually used in the meeting house, but it was doubtless the same one which was mentioned in 1654 in an inventory of the town property as "the towne clock at good Prats" and again in a similar inventory of 1657 as "a clock at John Allyns."

Another early instance of a privately owned clock in Hartford occurs in the inventory of Rev. Thomas Hooker in 1649. (The Connecticut Historical Society owns a fine tall clock with anchor escapement and seconds pendulum, made in London by Robert Markham and labelled as having been the property of Rev. Thomas Hooker. The seconds pendulum had not been invented at the time of Hooker's death; the anchor escapement was not developed until about 1680; tall clocks were first made about 1660, and Markham was, according to Britten, living and making clocks in London "behind the Exchange," in 1736-1740, nearly a hundred years after Hooker's death.) In 1659 the inventory of Governor Thomas Welles of Hartford listed a clock valued at one pound. The Hooker and Welles clocks, like that of Henry Packs, were undoubtedly brass lantern clocks made in England and imported by their owners. It was at least seventy-five years later before clocks were actually made in Hartford, and almost a hundred years before the town possessed a public clock in the steeple of the meeting house. That the ownership of a clock was far from usual in these pioneer days is shown by the comparatively small number of inventories which mention such an item. Samuel Stone, Hooker's successor as pastor of the Hartford church, had only an hour glass at the time of his death in 1663.

Owing to the fact that newspapers were not published in Connecticut until after the middle of the eighteenth century, there are few exact contemporary records, other than the surviving examples of the clocks themselves, of the precise character and scope of work which the earliest local clockmakers were prepared to undertake, and it is easy in the absence of such records, to assume that their activities were restricted to simple repairing and perhaps the attempted construction of a few crude timekeepers. It is certain however that their abilities were not different from those of their Pennsylvania, New York and Massachusetts contemporaries, and a review of the earliest issues of the *Boston News Letter* shows that most of the types and varieties of clocks (aside from the very elaborate automaton, art and astronomical clocks) which were ordinarily made in England, were also produced in Boston during the early eighteenth century. The advertisement in 1707 of James Batterson, clockmaker from London, read, "If any person - - - hath any occasion for New Clocks, or to have old ones turn'd into Pendelums; or any other thing either in making or mending; let them repair to the Sign of the Clock Dial at the South Side of the Town-House in Boston, where they may have them done at reasonable Rates." In 1712 Joseph Essex advertised in the *News Letter* "30 hour clocks, week clocks, month clocks, spring table clocks, chime clocks, quarter clocks, quarter chime clocks, church clocks, territ clocks, pocket watches and repeating watches" as being made in his shop in King Street, Boston.

From the advertisement of Joseph Essex it is clear that the colonial clockmaker of 1712 made at least three distinct types of clocks, the tower clock, the weight driven tall clock and the spring-driven table or shelf clock. These were all brass movement clocks of the contemporary English designs. There is every reason to believe that when Ebenezer Parmele began clockmaking in Connecticut in 1712 he was capable of executing substantially the same class of work. There is a definite record that he built a tower clock about 1726 and that his nephew and apprentice Abel Parmele was making brass eight-day repeating clocks prior to 1741. While no contemporary records refer to the wooden clock, it is almost certain that such clocks were being made by the earliest Connecticut clockmakers. The wooden clock was essentially a rural product, apparently not often made in the larger towns, but very generally favored by the farmers and small village yeomen. Macock Ward made such clocks in Wallingford, no doubt as early as 1725, and it is probable that Ebenezer Parmele himself was making them shortly after 1712.

The great majority of clocks made in America during the eighteenth century were tall case clocks, weight-driven, pendulum-controlled, with anchor escapements and hour strike. The details of the mechanisms and the designs of the dials followed very closely the styles popular in England. Prior to 1730 the square brass dial with frosted center, cast-brass corner ornaments, silvered ring and steel hands was the prevailing design. The arched dial followed, still with corner ornaments and silvered ring. In 1773 the engraved brass dial without frosting, ornaments or ring was introduced, and by 1790 the white-enameled iron dial became popular, although brass dials continued to find a place on the better clocks until at least the end of the century. The printed-paper and the painted-wooden dials were sometimes used with wooden movements as early as 1790, but they did not achieve real popularity until after the turn of the century, and even then were probably never fitted to anything but the cheapest wooden clocks.

Following English practice, the eighteenth century Connecticut brass clock dials were usually engraved with the maker's name and place of business. Occasionally the purchaser of the clock would indulge his ego to the extent of having his own name in addition to that of the clockmaker placed upon the dial, but apparently this custom was not widely prevalent. Britten, writing of conditions in England, notes that "on some of the early clocks the name inscribed was that of the owner. Between 1775 and 1825 the custom of having the name of the owner and not of the maker was often reverted to, usually with A.D. preceding the date figures, and occasionally also 'aged 21' or 'married' or 'born.' " Apparently few Connecticut clocks were thus marked with the owner's but not the clockmaker's names, although an occasional instance of the practice has been noticed.

The common belief that the early repairmen sometimes engraved their names on clocks which they were employed to clean or repair has probably no foundation in fact. No instances of such a custom have been discovered, although the desire to carry the date of a cherished heirloom further back than the name on the dial would permit has sometimes resulted in family traditions telling of the engraving of the repairman's name on the clock long after it came into the possession of the original reputed owner. Such traditions are invariably worthless.

In the early years of the nineteenth century, after the decline of the individual craftsmen and the rise of the clock factories, some of the names placed on the dials of the better class of clocks were those of dealers who sold clocks rather than those of the clockmakers. During the eighteenth century, however, American clocks were usually "bespoke" or made to order, and very few dealers carried them in stock. Such clocks were customarily secured directly from the local maker without the intervention of a dealer, and so far as is now known, none of the Connecticut clocks made during the eighteenth century show the names of dealers who sold but did not make them.

A word of caution relative to the marks, found on some clock movements, is in order, for many a late eighteenth century American made movement fitted with an enameled metal dial has been incorrectly attributed to an English maker owing to the fact that the false iron dial-plate upon which the dial itself is mounted often shows an English name and address. This is due to the fact that such dials and plates were usually imported and were marked according to British law with the name of the actual manufacturer. Apparently the art of enameling metal dials was not practiced in Connecticut. Such dials are, however, often seen carrying a Connecticut maker's name, but close inspection will usually show that the name was an addition to a previously completed dial. The difficulty and the unsatisfactory results attending the addition of a name to an enameled dial is responsible for the fact that large numbers of clocks having such dials are found without the clockmaker's name. Inspection of some of the Willard patent timepieces is instructive on this point, as many of these clocks clearly show the imported dial on a domestic movement. In some instances it is possible that Connecticut clockmakers may have directly imported enameled dials made up with their names neatly lettered by the foreign dial maker.

In general the presence of an imported enameled dial does not of itself indicate that the clock movement was or was not imported, as these dials were very frequently carried in stock by dealers in hardware and clockmakers' supplies and were sold to clockmakers throughout the country.

The possibility that the name on an old clock dial may be a forgery must not be overlooked. This is a serious matter in the instances of the more famous early English clockmakers, as many forgeries of the work of Windmills, Tompion, Quare and Harrison have been made, but it is probably not as yet a question of great importance in Connecticut clocks, since so little is known of the earlier Connecticut makers that there has been small incentive for outright forgery. Undoubtedly, however, old or reproductions of old movements of one maker have been fitted with dials of another and placed in cases of unknown date and paternity in order to assemble an antique. When this has been done by an expert equipped with an accurate knowledge of the subject, the fraud is extremely difficult to detect.

As has been previously noted, the clockmakers often sold clock movements without the cases, the latter being secured from an independent cabinet-maker. In some few instances (particularly where the clock movement was a cheap wooden one) the purchaser may have temporarily hung it high up on the wall and used it for a time without a case, thus giving rise to the so-called "wag-on-the-wall," but the manifest disadvantages of exposed pendulum and weights, to say nothing of the effect of dirt on the mechanism, made this a rare and invariably a temporary expedient, resorted to only by the poorest farmers pending the time when they could make or secure a simple case in which to house the mechanism. The wag-on-the-wall (as differentiated from the early imported brass lantern clock with pendulum) was therefore not a distinct type of Connecticut clock, but was merely the uncased movement of an ordinary tall clock. The better grades of brass movements were probably never treated in this fashion, while comparatively few even of the cheapest wooden clocks were used without cases.

Occasionally a tall clock is found carrying a paper label which identifies the cabinet-maker who furnished the case. Probably not one eighteenth century clock case in a thousand is thus labeled, and it is advisable to use the greatest caution in accepting such identification as authentic, since the increasing demand from collectors for signed examples of early cabinet work will inevitably lead to the forging of labels.

CHAPTER III: BRASS CLOCKMAKING

HE most important products of the eighteenth century clock shops were brass movement domestic clocks, and by far the greater number of these were eight-day striking tall clocks. A calendar attachment was commonly included and was probably of almost as much utility as the minute hand, for printed calendars were unknown at that period and an almanac was not always available. The moon phase attachment had a similar if more limited practical value and was often applied to the earlier clocks. Repeaters and musical clocks were but expensive sophistications which appealed to a limited number of wealthy purchasers. Aside from the tall clocks, a very few bracket and wall clocks with brass movements were produced in Connecticut as early as 1775, although the springs, fuzees, fuzee chains, and perhaps other components of these clocks were doubtless imported.

The early brass clocks were always made of castings, hence the wheels and plates were invariably heavy and substantial. It was not until about 1837 that sheet brass was generally used for plates and wheels, necessitating a complete revision of manufacturing methods and reducing both the price and the quality of metal clocks to a level comparable with the wooden clock.

No attempt need here be made to discuss the detailed design of clock movements. That subject is highly technical and complex, an extensive literature (of interest primarily to the trade) covers every phase of it, and the Connecticut craftsmen of the period under consideration made no important contributions to it. The brass clock was essentially European in conception and design, a relatively standardized piece of mechanism significant chiefly from the fact that it occupied such an important place in the domestic economy of the eighteenth century, that it was much the most intricate machine in common use, and that the technique of its production involved the extreme limits of craft skill and precision in a day of comparatively simple things.

The early American craftsmen were not inventors or improvers of clock mechanisms. On the contrary, they adhered strictly to the details of construction and styles of ornamentation current in the mother country. No doubt there was an appreciable delay after an innovation appeared in England before it was adopted in the colonies, and this was particularly true of conditions in Connecticut, where prior to the Revolutionary War very few European trained clockmakers had settled. It was largely due to the efforts of Thomas Harland, the English trained immigrant, and his apprentices that musical clocks were made in significant numbers in the State and that the flat engraved and silvered brass dial was popularized. Toward the end of the century the inventive faculty began to show itself in the Connecticut clockmakers. Benjamin Hanks patented his self-winding tower clock in 1783, Eli Terry his equation clock in 1797, and Simeon Jocelin his "silent moving time piece" in 1800. From that time to the present, the Connecticut clockmakers have made innumerable detail improvements in simplifying and reducing the cost of clocks, but it must be confessed that no advance in the art comparable to the basic inventions of the fuzee, pendulum, hair-spring, anchor escapement or chronometer has been originated in America.

The early clockmaker made most of the tools with which he worked. The construction of these tools formed a part of his apprentice training and there is little doubt that a self-made tool kit formed his principal capital at the time when he left his master's shop a full-fledged journeyman. Toward the end of the craftsman century, however, tools were imported in considerable variety and the necessity for making them diminished, so that by 1800 no difficulty would have been encountered in purchasing a complete complement of clockmaking equipment from local merchants. Even as early as 1725 some of the more common tools of general utility could be purchased locally, and it is probable that a few of them found their way into the clockmaker's shop. The fact that Daniel Burnap as late as 1785 made his lathes, taps and dividers, but purchased his engravers' and joiners' tools, is indicative of the necessity for home construction of the more specialized clockmaking equipment.

The newspapers of the eighteenth century throw considerable light on the possible sources from which the Connecticut clockmakers may have procured tools. The advertisements in these papers show that in 1716 Samuel Bissel of Newport, Rhode Island, an anvil-smith from England, was making "all sorts of Black-smith's and Gold-smith's anvils," that in 1732 William Bryant of Boston was making smiths' vises as well as carpenters' and braziers' tools of various kinds, and that in 1741 Joseph Clough of Boston was a maker of bellows for furnaces, refiners, blacksmiths, braziers and goldsmiths. In 1765 James Tilley of Hartford was offering for sale "an assortment of files suitable for silversmiths and jewelers," in 1771 Jonathan Trott of Boston advertised in the *New London Gazette* "imported fine and coarse files, melting pots, &c.," John Breed of Norwich was offering "bellows, Hand saws, Carpenters and Joiners tools, scales and dividers," and Joseph Gale, also of Norwich, had for sale "Carpenters and Joiners tools, Files and rasps, Gimblets, Tapborers, Handsaws and Bellows." In 1772 Abel Buell the versatile goldsmith of New Haven had for sale large and small files, round and flat steel pliers, cutting nippers, spring dividers, tweezers, large and small draw plates, bench and hand vises, watch tale vises, blow pipes, drill bows and steel gravers. In 1773 John Champlin, the New London silversmith advertised "materials for repairing Clocks and Watches," in 1792 Thomas Hilldrup of Hartford was offering numerous imported watchmaker's tools such as screw plates, pliers, saws, vises, broaches, drills and hammers, in 1794 Beach & Ward of Hartford were selling "elegant Engines for Clock and Watch makers," and by 1802 Ward was offering "Sets of Cast Clock Work, Clock and Watchmakers Files, Clock Glasses and dial plates, pinions, hands and bells." The day of the "assembled" clock had arrived.

It is fortunately possible to reconstruct the eighteenth century clock shop and to learn in detail the nature of the tools with which the clockmaker worked. Such information is contained in the itemized inventories of the estates of the deceased craftsmen. The earliest Connecticut clockmaker's inventory which has been found is that of Hezekiah Hotchkiss in 1761, and the next are those of John Whitear, Jr., and Samuel Rockwell in 1773. The fact that some of the actual tools are still in existence makes it possible to be specific in describing their character and use.

In the construction of a brass clock movement, the eighteenth century clockmaker used scrap brass which he remelted in a small crucible set in his forge fire. A hand bellows was used to force the temperature of the fire up to the melting point of the metal, when the crucible was removed with a pair of crucible tongs and its contents was poured into a previously prepared mold.

The mold was made up in a flask, patterns being used in exactly the same manner in which they are still employed by foundrymen. Wood patterns were probably common, although metal patterns were by no means unknown as will be noted by referring to the inventory of Isaac Doolittle, where such patterns are specifically mentioned.

When the casting had solidified the flask was opened, the casting removed and allowed to become perfectly cold, and it was then cleaned and smoothed up with a file preparatory to hammering.

Since the casting as it came from the mold was soft and entirely unsuited for use as a clock wheel or plate, the clockmaker subjected it to a process of cold working or hammering in order to stiffen and refine the metal. The piece was held in a pair of tongs, laid upon a smooth faced anvil and hammered to the desired degree. This operation was considered important, Hatton in 1773 remarking that "hammering is a great qualification" and "therefore every boy ought to be taught the art of hammering with great care; and to obtain which he should practice well on clock dials." Wheels and plates were hammered only enough to develop the requisite degree of toughness, but dials were necessarily given a much more prolonged hammering with intermediate annealing in the forge to avoid cracking the metal. While plates and wheels were hammered to secure toughness, dials were hammered to reduce and spread the metal into a thin sheet, the latter operation—a lengthy and laborious one—being followed by polishing, engraving and chemical silvering to complete the dial.

The clock plates, having been cast and hammered, were next made true and smooth with a file. A great deal of the clockmaker's work was done with files and it is doubtful whether any other mechanics have ever equaled the skill of the early craftsmen with these tools. During the operation of filing, the piece was held in a substantial iron vise mounted on the work bench with jaws at the level of the elbow of the worker, who customarily stood at his work. Unusual care was taken to line up the vise so that its jaws would be exactly in vertical and horizontal planes, this being done to insure accurate filing, since the art of filing was almost entirely one of touch, and correct location of the work was a necessary preliminary to uniformity of results.

Having thus completed the blanks for the plates, the next step was the locating and drilling of the various holes for the pillars, pivots and screws. The locations for these holes were transferred from a drawing or "calibre" of the movement which had previously been laid out by the clockmaker, in many cases, no doubt, during his apprenticeship. This drawing was usually made with scriber and dividers upon a thin piece of metal. In transferring the locations of the holes from the calibre to the clock frame, dividers were used, the holes carefully transferred and their positions scratched upon the smooth surface of the plate casting.

To drill the holes in the plates a bow drill was employed, perhaps the first tool ever invented by prehistoric man. The drilled holes were then broached with an iron broach in order to smooth and harden the metal, and the plate was finally given a careful polishing with a piece of wood charged with tripoli.

The hammered castings for wheels were carefully filed and the outside diameters and bores were finished in the lathe, one of the important machines in the clockmaker's shop.

The clockmaker's lathe was made of wrought iron or brass. The tailstock was adjustable along the bed and both the headstock and tailstock centers were adjustable longitudinally. Neither center rotated however, the work to be turned being supported by the centers and caused to rotate by means of a small wood pulley which turned freely upon the headstock center. This pulley was turned by a gut or leather band from a wooden handwheel operated by the left hand of the worker. The pulley was provided with a pin in its side which engaged a small dog clamped to the piece of work. The machine was thus perfectly adapted to producing very accurate work in spite of the fact that the workmanship of the lathe itself was comparatively crude. Turning tools were of steel, mounted in wooden handles. When in use they were supported on an adjustable tool rest and manipulated entirely by the right hand of the worker. A large iron lathe was about fourteen inches long over the bed and a small one about eight inches long. These lathes were supported in wooden blocks fastened to the work bench, or were held in the jaws of a vise. The wheels, having been turned and trued in the lathe, were then mounted in the wheel cutting engine, and the teeth were cut.

The clockmaker's engine was the most elaborate of his tools. It was a device of the highest significance in the history of metal working machinery for it was the direct ancestor of the present day milling machines and gear cutters. Prior to 1655, the teeth of clock wheels were marked off with a radial ruler swinging on a pin fastened to the center of a circular protractor and were filed out by hand. About the year 1655 Robert Hook, F.R.S., designed the wheel cutting engine with a dividing plate, index pin, work arbor and revolving milling cutter, a machine which was promptly adopted by the clockmakers and no doubt formed an essential part of the equipment of the earliest American craftsmen. As time went on, improvements were made in the engine. Perhaps the most widely used model during the latter half of the eighteenth century was that designed by John Wyke of Lancaster, England, (b. 1720—d. 1787), one of whose machines is preserved in the Science Museum, South Kensington, England. Machines of this type were imported into America, but many of the Connecticut craftsmen used engines of domestic make. These latter were essentially copies of the English machines but instead of being made wholly of metal they were usually built up on a mahogany base and were of less durable construction and somewhat cruder in details than the English models. A majority of the American made engines were the product of the clockmakers themselves, one of the tasks of an advanced apprentice being apparently the making of an engine for his own use.

A wheel cutting engine which was used in Connecticut in 1780 is illustrated on Plate 5. An identical machine was owned by John Avery and is now in the possession of Mr. James E. Conlon of Boston. The machines were of course hand operated, but the basic principles were thoroughly sound and many of these principles were subsequently elaborated by Joseph Brown of Providence in his earliest gear cutting and power milling machines.

While engines of this kind were typical of the state of the art both in Europe and America during the eighteenth century, it is recorded that a greatly improved machine was built by Henry Hindley, a clockmaker of York, England, as early as 1740. Hindley's engine was provided with a worm and wheel for indexing, a divided plate, and a sector, and was by many years the forerunner of the modern milling machine index head. Apparently, however, this improved machine was unknown in America until long after 1800.

The wheel cutting engine simply divided and cut the spaces between the wheel teeth but did not shape the tops of the teeth. This operation, known as "rounding up," was done with a file while the wheel was held in the bench vise. After "rounding up" the teeth, the wheel was polished by hand and was then ready to be mounted on its pinion.

Pinions were made of wrought iron or steel. They were forged out roughly on the anvil, cut to length with a small hand saw, turned to the proper size in the lathe, the teeth cut by hand with a file, hardened in the forge fire, and polished by hand with tripoli and rouge.

Screws were made in screw plates or (in the case of the larger sizes) in the lathe. A screw plate was a flat piece of steel having a number of threaded holes tapped through it, each hole being progressively smaller than the preceding one. The screw blank, after being turned down to the proper diameter, and slightly pointed and a slot sawed in the head, was twisted into a hole in the screw plate a trifle smaller than the diameter of the blank. The action was a squeezing or compression of the material, and by this means a thread was formed (rather than cut) upon the screw blank. Radial notches were often filed in the sides of the holes in screw plates, thus converting them into semblances of thread cutting dies, but as these notches were ordinarily not sharpened, they served chiefly as a means of concentrating the pressure and making the forming of the thread somewhat easier, rather than as real cutting points.

Original taps and large screws for which the screw plate was unsuited were cut with a file in the lathe, the file being held and guided at the proper angle entirely by hand. The fineness of the file was proportioned to the size of the thread, and very fine threads used in watch work were cut with a knife edge held and guided in the same manner as the file.

The small parts entering into the construction of the clock movement were made chiefly with files, the bow drill and the lathe. Pillars were brass castings turned in the lathe, hands were usually made of iron or steel, pierced with the drill and filed to shape, pallets were forged, filed to shape, hardened and polished, and assembling of the parts was done at the bench with a file and hammer as the chief accessories.

The use of gages for arriving at the correct shapes for clock parts was well known to the early makers. Thus Hatton in 1773 wrote, "It only remains now to show the method by which the hyperbola is to be described in order to make a gauge for giving the true form of the fuzee required in any particular case," and after explaining the geometrical construction of the curve he adds, "When the curve is thus drawn on paper it will be easy to transfer it to a plate of brass or steel, and thereby (to make) a gauge for giving the true figure to the fuzee."

Clockmakers frequently drew their own wire. A piece of iron was forged out into a small bar on the anvil, pointed, and then drawn with tongs through a wire plate or die held in the vise. This tool was a hardened steel plate perforated with a number of bell-mouthed holes of various diameters. The wire was pulled successively through holes of diminishing diameters until the correct size for the purpose at hand was reached.

It is hardly an exaggeration to say that the eighteenth century clockmaker could carry his entire equipment upon his back and that every piece of it was well within his ability to make for himself.

CHAPTER IV: WOOD CLOCKMAKING

VERY little is known of the history of the wooden clock. The wood clock was not, as has sometimes been implied, an American development. It was being made in Europe as far back as the seventeenth century and probably originated in Germany or Holland. In any event it was well known in England by the year 1700 and perhaps much earlier. Harrison (of chronometer fame) made such clocks in his youth, and several of them, dating from about 1713, are still preserved. Wooden watch movements of the general character of the so-called Nuremberg Eggs were made in Germany at a very early date, one interesting example, provided with ivory wheels, being owned by the Deutsches Museum.

Unfortunately no records of any kind have been found to definitely date the introduction of the earliest type of wooden clock into Connecticut. The Fitch manuscripts mention the making of wooden clocks as common in East Hartford in 1761 and imply that the trade was then held in small repute. Macock Ward's tools clearly indicate that he made wooden clocks and it may legitimately be inferred that his knowledge of them dated to his apprenticeship under Parmele in the years 1715-1720. Of Parmele, so little is known that it becomes a matter of pure guesswork to suggest that he in turn may have secured a knowledge of the wooden clock from the Dutch craftsman in New York under whom he is presumed to have served his apprenticeship in 1705-1710. Such an unsupported hypothesis would nevertheless account for the early appearance and spread of wood clock-making in Connecticut, since all of the earliest known makers of these clocks in the colony can be traced by direct inference to Parmele. The fact that Parmele was a versatile worker in wood lends some additional color to the supposition that he may have been acquainted with the wooden clock.

The early type of wooden movement is very rare, and is almost unknown outside of Hartford County. It is characterized by heavy construction, rough workmanship and large lenticular wheels with hand-cut teeth. Nearly all of these movements were originally fitted with high grade brass dials and were cased in handsome cases. They are sometimes referred to as "Cheney movements" since they were made by several members of that family, but the real origin of the design is unknown. This type of wooden movement was the only one made in Connecticut prior to about the year 1790, and it continued to be produced as late as 1812 although largely superseded before 1800 by the later style of movement so commonly seen in the unlabelled tall clocks of the early nineteenth century. An early wood movement made, probably about 1760, by Timothy Cheney, is shown on Plate 6. It may be considered as perfectly representative of the Connecticut wood clock prior to 1790.

The late type of wooden clock, which appeared in the state about 1790, is thought to have been introduced by Gideon Roberts of Bristol. One of Roberts' clocks, made about 1800 is illustrated on Plate 7. Prior to 1790 Roberts had lived in the Wyoming Valley in Pennsylvania and had undoubtedly become familiar with the wooden clocks produced by the German settlers of that region, clocks which were similar in design to the later Connecticut models. The entire matter is obscure to say the least, and the only perfectly safe statement is that wooden clocks were being made in Connecticut certainly prior to 1750, probably by 1725, and possibly as early as 1712.

The wooden movement was peculiarly adaptable to the pioneer conditions in Connecticut. It was cheap, the materials oak, apple, laurel and cherry were abundant native woods, and the technique of sawing, planing and turning the parts was of the simplest nature, requiring but the common carpenters' hand tools and a primitive wooden foot lathe. Most of the brass clocks of the eighteenth century were made with seconds pendulum and weight drive, and the wooden movements were similarly designed, but owing to the far greater friction set up in the wood movement, the latter was usually made to run but thirty hours instead of eight days.

There are substantial reasons to believe that most of the earliest Connecticut clockmakers were called upon to make wooden clocks. Examples of early eighteenth century work are, however, excessively rare. This is not surprising in view of the fragile nature of these clocks and the fact that they were never held in particularly high esteem. Wooden wheels were satisfactory for some years of service, but as the wood dried out, a tendency developed for the teeth to split off along the grain. Pivot holes in wood wore away, and both heat and cold, as well as dampness affected the plates and wheels, causing warping and cracking. Many of the early wood movements were doubtless replaced by others of later date, and in some instances it is even possible that brass movements may have taken the place of worn out wooden ones.

Throughout the eighteenth century the methods used in making wood movements were substantially those of the cabinet-maker. The tools were a hand saw and plane, bow drill or hand brace, file, knife, compass and foot lathe. The plates were usually made of oak, split, planed smooth, sawed out by hand and drilled for the pillars and pivots with a hand drill. Wheels were of cherry, planed to thickness, marked out with a compass, the teeth stepped off with dividers and the wheels sawed out with a fine saw, the teeth being finally smoothed up with a file. Arbors, barrels and pillars were turned in a foot operated pole lathe similar to that used for turning the parts of spinning wheels and furniture. Hands were cast or filed, and dials were identical with those used on the brass clocks, although by the end of the century printed-paper and painted-wooden dials were used in imitation of the white-enameled dials found on the better grades of clocks of the period. The weights, of about eight pounds, were usually made of rough iron castings or, toward the end of the century, of thin sheet iron cans filled with sand. The pendulum rod was either a wooden rod or an iron wire flattened with a hammer at one end and tempered to form the spring, and the pendulum bob was a lead or iron casting faced with a brass shell.

Up to the year 1800, the wood movement was a hand-made product, and no attempt was made by the clockmakers to improve the technical methods of its production. Possibly templates may have been used for marking out wheels and locating pivot holes in plates, for the movements show a degree of uniformity which suggests that the makers employed patterns as guides.

It has repeatedly been stated that the teeth of the wheels in the early wood movements were cut on some type of wheel cutting engine. The clockmakers were of course well acquainted with the engine used for gashing out the teeth of brass wheels, and all of them who made brass clocks owned these machines, but the brass wheel cutting engine was poorly adapted to cutting the wood wheel with its wide face, straight-sided triangular teeth, coarse pitch and large diameter. Apparently it was not until about 1800 or shortly afterward that wood wheels were first actually cut by machinery. Eli Terry is said to have devised a machine for the purpose. Gideon Roberts and John Rich were both provided with machines for cutting wooden wheel teeth and pinions before 1812, and in 1814 Asa Hopkins patented the well-known three spindle machine for this work, a machine which, with but slight changes, is still in use for cutting certain classes of sheet brass wheels.

In point of numbers, it is possible that more wooden than brass clocks were made in Connecticut during the eighteenth century. According to the contemporary account of Fitch, Benjamin Cheney was devoting himself entirely to the wooden clock in 1761, while his brother Timothy made both types. In 1786 the rural community of Lebanon, Connecticut, boasted of thirteen wooden clocks and only seven brass ones, although in 1794 the larger and more prosperous town of Guilford contained thirty-five wooden clocks and fifty-four brass ones. The early wood clocks were all of the tall case variety, and it was not until 1815 that the first wood movement shelf clock was made.

The eighteenth century wood clocks almost invariably carried the makers' names on the dials, but on the factory-made wooden tall clocks of the first two decades of the nineteenth century these names were often omitted. In general therefore, it is safe to assume that an unmarked clock of this type is a late product.

CHAPTER V: PUBLIC CLOCKS

TOWER clocks were made in Connecticut from 1727 on through the eighteenth century. The actual number of such clocks constructed was of course comparatively small, but many of the clockmakers undertook to supply the limited demand. By the middle of the century a significant number of Connecticut churches could boast of clocks made in the colony, and during the later years several of the better-known clockmakers advertised their readiness to make clocks of this kind. Of these late eighteenth century makers of tower clocks, perhaps the most prominent were Harland, Enos Doolittle, Jocelin, Burnap, Hanks, Blakslee and Terry.

The early church clocks were not often purchased by the ecclesiastical societies, but were usually secured by public subscription, and permission was granted to the subscribers to install the clocks in the meeting houses without direct cost to the societies. The records are meager, but they seem to warrant the belief that this procedure was an ingenious scheme of the clockmakers to further the sale of their clocks. One can readily imagine the clockmaker quietly agitating the subject of a town clock, circulating a subscription paper headed perhaps by donations from a few of the leading men of the town and urging the less willing to contribute their quota of bills, hard money or country produce to the good cause. Eventually the necessary amount would be pledged and "liberty" would be secured to present the clock to the town. That such "liberty" was cheerfully granted seems evident, but the town fathers were sometimes more than cautious, as in 1738, when giving Macock Ward the requested permission to place a tower clock in the Wallingford meeting house they carefully specified that if any damage resulted to the steeple, he was to make it good and remove the clock.

In the seventeenth and the early years of the eighteenth centuries the term "town clock" was not always synonymous with "tower clock." The late Dr. I. W. Lyon considered that the earliest Boston town clocks were lantern clocks used by the bell ringers to indicate the time for ringing the bells in the meeting houses. As has been previously pointed out, the earliest Hartford town clock was unquestionably of this character since the records show that it was kept for various periods in different private houses in the village. The clock in Wethersfield prior to 1749 may also have been of the same kind although in this instance the records are not decisive.

It is probable that most, if not all of the early tower clocks erected in Connecticut were made in the colony. Their quality was not always above criticism. The faults of the Hartford town clock were fully aired in the *Courant* in 1790, and the Wethersfield clock, installed in 1749, must have been something less than perfect in view of the great care taken in 1784 to insure that the new clock authorized at that time should be a creditable piece of work.

Guilford was probably the first town in the colony to be provided with a tower clock. In 1726 a steeple and bell were added to the meeting house, and on December 20, 1726, liberty was "granted to any of the Inhabitants of this parish to set up & fix a suitable Clock in the meeting house, with a hammer to strike on the great bell;—provided the Charge of purchasing sd. clock be raised by voluntary contribution." The clock was made by Ebenezer Parmele, duly installed in the belfry, and for many years was wound up and kept in repair by its maker. A tower clock movement, said to be this original Parmele clock, is preserved in the Historical Museum at Guilford.

In Wethersfield the "keeping and repairing of the clock and bell" was a Society charge in 1734, and in 1741 Thomas Fox was paid thirty pounds for this work. In 1749, however, it was voted that "a public clock shall be procured by subscription and the subscribers shall have liberty to set it in the meeting house, and after that it shall be maintained at cost of said Society." In March 1784 it was voted to have a new bell and a "good clock, equal to that now in Farmington Old Society, with three faces." The clock was put in place in 1791 but was not accepted until a formal report had been made at the Society's request by David Lowrey that it was "good, strong and well constructed, and fully equal to that in Farmington Society."

On December 5, 1738, the town of Wallingford voted: "The town gives liberty to Mecok Ward to sett a clok in ye steeple; and if any damadge to ye belfre; hee will pay it and taik away ye clok." In this same year a clock was authorized for the meeting house in Farmington.

In 1740 Ebenezer Parmele built a brass tower clock for the meeting house in Milford. This was apparently constructed upon the order of the town and not purchased by subscription. It remained in use until 1825, when it was replaced by a wood clock built by Barzilla Davidson. Some thirteen years later, in 1838, E. R. Lambert, in commenting on the new wood clock wrote: "If the new wooden clock could have the moving power attached to it that Redheifer once fixed to his perpetual motion in Philadelphia, viz. an old negro behind the curtain to turn it, perhaps it might answer a better purpose than at present."

Norwich was provided with a meeting house clock in 1745, said to have cost eight pounds exclusive of fixtures, and shortly afterwards a clock and bell were placed in Christ Church, Stratford. The bell was cast by John Whitear, and it is altogether probable that he also furnished the clock.

An engraving made in 1749, purporting to show the Yale College building in New Haven, illustrates a large single hand clock projecting from a central dormer window of the building, but it is improbable that such a clock was in existence at the time. The engraving in question, made by Thomas Johnston from a drawing by Greenwood, is notoriously inaccurate in many respects, and it is now generally held by antiquarians that the clock was purely imaginary. The college records of the period make no reference to the clock. The engraving is nevertheless of interest in that it shows a style of clock dial frequently used at that date. Prior to 1785 the college was in possession of a clock. A print of the college buildings published in that year by Daniel Bowen in New Haven shows a single hand clock in the tower of the college chapel, and in 1786 President Stiles noted in his diary that one of the college servants was allowed fifty shillings a year for "winding up the clock."

The first tower clock in Hartford is said to have been purchased by public subscription in 1752 and placed in the steeple of the meeting house. Here it seems to have remained until the early years of the nineteenth century when the old meeting house was replaced by the present Center Church. During the period of construction of the new building the clock was stored in Christ Church belfry, but was returned to the Center Church when the latter was completed, and apparently continued in use until 1849 when a new clock was installed at a cost of seven hundred dollars. An interesting commentary on the original clock was printed in the *Courant* on July 19, 1790:

"A correspondent wishes to know why the Town Clock in Hartford is not kept in better repair, and more regular. It is of consequence not only to Courts and public meetings, but to private families and laboring men, that a public clock should keep true time. Yet the town clock in Hartford varies every week from a quarter to a half an hour from true time. A man therefore who has a good time piece, must keep different hours from his neighbors, or a good time piece will be useless to him. It is a very easy thing to keep the clock in order, and to a large town is a very great convenience."

PART TWO

CLOCKMAKERS

OF

EIGHTEENTH CENTURY CONNECTICUT

SEVENTY-NINE CLOCKMAKERS

HE precise details of the lives of the early clockmakers are not easy to discover. Many of these men were but obscure village artizans, oppressed by poverty and large families. Only occasionally did they achieve sufficient local prominence to warrant more than a passing mention of their names in the annals of their times. A few of the late and more progressive among them made extensive use of advertisements, most of them left enduring records in the shape of the clocks which they constructed and the town and church records of their communities usually reveal the critical dates in their lives.

What is known of this group of craftsmen is here recorded for the benefit of the student of early American craftsmanship and the collector of clocks. That the list is incomplete is certain. No excuse is necessary for the extensive reprinting of the early advertisements and inventories, for it is material of this kind which ultimately reveals the true capabilities and accomplishments of these pioneer mechanics and throws genuine light upon a not wholly unimportant phase of colonial life in America.

The list is confined exclusively to men who were established in the business prior to the year 1800. Very few craftsmen entered the trade after that time, although creditable work was done by Judah Hart of Middletown and Norwich, Nathanial Olmsted of Farmington and New Haven, the firm of Heydorn & Imlay (1808-

1811) in Hartford, the firm of Sibley & Marble (1801-1806) in New Haven, and by a few others.

APOCRYPHA

MUCH of the information hitherto available concerning the Connecticut clockmakers is unreliable. A comparison of the dates of birth and death of some of the men listed in these notes with the dates ascribed to them in several of the works on clockmaking will illustrate the incorrectness of not a few such ascribed dates. The practice of assigning but a single date when more complete data can be found is to be discouraged on the ground that it sometimes fosters grave misconceptions and occasionally results in errors in dating by as much as fifty years. Actual instances of such errors have occurred in the labeling of well-known public collections.

Anyone familiar with the modern lists of American clockmakers contained in recent popular books on the subject will notice the omission from the present study of several names heretofore believed to have been those of eighteenth century Connecticut craftsmen. David Aird of Middletown, J. Cheeny of East Hartford, Thomas Hilldrup and Isaac Sanford of Hartford, Nathaniel Jocelin and James Joslyn of New Haven, and Thomas Sadd of East Windsor are none of them entitled to inclusion in such lists for the simple reason that not one of them ever made a clock.

David Aird was a professional thief who masqueraded at one time in Middletown as a clock- and watch-maker, but there is no reason to suppose that he carried on the trades. On November 8, 1785, he advertised:

> David Aird, Watch-Maker from London, Begs leave to inform the Public, that he carries on the Clock and Watch-making business in all its Branches, at the second Door North of the Printing Office.
>
> N. B. Some Delays have been made, occasioned by Want of Tools necessary to carry on the Trade. And as he has received the proper Tools, flatters himself that he shall be able to perform the Work with Dispatch.

Shortly after the appearance of this advertisement, Aird absconded, and on January 3, 1786, the *Middlesex Gazette* remarked editorially:

> David Aird, who has advertised himself as Watch Maker from London, has left this city without adjusting his accounts with his creditors. Persons who have entrusted him with watches or business of any kind, may perhaps do well to enquire after their property. 'Tis supposed that he feels conscious of the wrong he does his native city by depriving it, by his absence, of so useful a member of society, and has returned again to London.

The supposition that Aird had returned to London was evidently incorrect, for in August, 1787, he returned to Middletown and stole two china-faced watches from Amos Treadway. In advertising the theft, Treadway stated that Aird's real name was Charles Brewster, and that he was "a trancient person apt to change his name, 25 or 26 years old, 5 feet & 8 or 9 inches high, has an impediment in his speech when he attempts to speak quick. Has been in Gaol, whipt & rode the Wooden Horse at Hartford for Horse Stealing. Was a soldier in the late federal Regiment at Springfield."

J. Cheeny of East Hartford is merely a typographical error made in Britten's book and conscientiously copied into the subsequent compilations. The correct initial is T. and the man was Timothy Cheney.

Thomas Hilldrup was a jeweler and watch repairer and for some years was postmaster of Hartford. He made no clocks, a fact perfectly evident from his extensive advertisements and the inventory of his shop tools. He has sometimes been mentioned as a silversmith, but his advertisements and inventory tend to disprove the belief that he carried on that trade. He was an amusing and original character and no doubt contributed greatly to the gaiety of postrevolutionary Hartford. While he was a consistent advertiser, he met with small success, and died insolvent in 1795.

Nathaniel Jocelin of New Haven was a baker and confectioner, the father of Simeon Jocelin the clockmaker, but himself most certainly not a maker of clocks. James Joslyn is a figment of the imagination; Thomas Sadd was a physician, the father of Harvey Sadd, the clockmaker of New Hartford; and Isaac Sanford was an engraver, miniaturist and inventor, but not a clockmaker, although at one time in partnership with Miles Beach.

JOEL ATKINS, *Middletown*

(B. —D.)

The following advertisement appeared in the *Connecticut Gazette*, of New London, on February 14, 1777.

> Joel Atkins, Clock & Watch Maker, Having opened a Shop next South to Mrs. Bigelow's Tavern, in Middletown; takes this Method to acquaint those Gentlemen that want their Watches repaired, that they may have them done in the most reasonable Manner, with quick dispatch, and their Custom will oblige their humble Servant.
>
> Joel Atkins.

Nothing further is known of this man.

JOHN AVERY, *Preston*

(B. 1732—D. 1794)

John Avery, a son of John and Ann (Stanton) Avery, was born at Preston on December 6, 1732. He was one of a long line of John Averys, his father and grandfather, as well as his son and grandson, having the same name. On January 22, 1752, he married Mary Parke, and following her death in 1769 he married Experience Stanton and became the father of fourteen children. He was a farmer, goldsmith and clockmaker who lived on the east side of Avery Pond in a homestead which is still standing. He was a justice of the peace for many years, and in 1774 and 1775 was a selectman of Preston. He was successively an ensign and a lieutenant of the train band of Preston in 1774. At the outbreak of the Revolutionary War he procured a paid substitute, but in 1776 the general assembly made him a member of "the Committee appointed to procure and purchase fire arms in this state." He died in Preston on July 23, 1794, leaving the following tools in his shop:

1	BRASS LATHE	18–0
1	GROOVING INSTRUMENT	6–0
1	LARGE INGOT	2–0
1	BENCH VISE	12–0
1	HAND VISE	3–0
1	SCREW PLATE & TAPS	5–0
1	WIRE PLATE	3–0
1	CLOCK FRAME	2–0
1	PAIR LARGE SHOP SHEARS	3–0
1	PAIR FURNACE TONGS	2–0
1	GOLDSMITHS TIN PAN	3–0
1	PAIR GREAT NIPPERS	2–0
1	RING SWAGE	2–0
2	PAIRS OLD PLIERS	1–0
1	RING PLATE	0–6
1	SWEEP FOR MAKING CLOCK	4–6
7	LATHE WHIRLS & ARBORS	3–0
1	BRASS BEAD BLOCK	3–0
1	NAIL HAMMER	1–0
1	OLD SMITHS HAMMER	1–0
1	SILVERSMITHS HAMMER	0–10
1	TINKERS HAMMER	0–9
3	FRAMING CHISELS	2–6
1	WIMBLE BIT	1–0
1	MACHINE FOR CUTTING OR GRINDING CRYSTALS & PIVOTS	2–14–0
1	SMALL SPOON SWAGE	1–0
1	SPOON MOULD	3–0
1	JEWEL HAMMER	0–6
5	BURNISHERS & BORERS	2–6
26	OLD FILES	10–0
	NUMBER OF SPOON & BUTTON PUNCHES	6–3
1	BLOW PIPE	0–9
1	TURNING CHISEL & GOUGE	2–0
	BEAD CUTTERS & PUNCHES	2–6
	BUTTON & JEWEL PUNCHES	9–0
1	GUN SCREW PLATE	1–3
1	SCALE STAMP	0–9
1	ENGINE FOR CUTTING CLOCK WHEELS	1–10–0
1	SMALL SCREW PLATE	1–0
	MONEY SCALES & WEIGHTS	9–0
1	PLATING MILL	1–10–0
1	BLOCK KNIFE	2–6
1	BLOCK GOUGE	2–6
1	HANDSAW	3–0
1	JOINTER & IRON	2–6
1	SMOOTHING PLANE & IRON	1–6
2	AUGERS	1–0
1	GOUGE	0–4
1	MORTISING AX	2–0
1	FROW	1–6
1	SPOON TEEST	22–0
1	BICK IRON, ANVIL & LARGE RING SWAGE	1–1–0
1	BUTTON MOULD	3–0

ELEAZER BAKER, *Ashford*

(B. 1764—D. 1849)

Eleazer Baker was born in Tolland on December 17, 1764, a son of Joseph Jr. and Lois Baker. On April 12, 1787 he married Hannah Trowbridge of Pomfret and settled in Ashford. In 1793 he advertised:

> Eleazer Baker Informs the public that he carries on the clock and watch making and goldsmith's business in all their various branches at his shop in Ashford. One or two apprentices about 15 or 16 years of age are wanted at the above business.

One of the apprentices taken at this time was Edmund Hughes who ran away in June of the following year and a number of years later appeared as a silversmith and clockmaker in Hampton and subsequently settled in Middletown.

Baker apparently died in Mansfield in 1849 at the age of seventy-five, having given up clockmaking many years previously.

EBENEZER BALCH, *Hartford & Wethersfield*
(B. 1723—D. 1808)

Ebenezer Balch, son of Joseph and Mary (Osgood) Balch was born in Boston on May 14, 1723 and learned the trades of clockmaking and silversmithing in his native town. Upon completing his apprenticeship, in 1744, he settled in Hartford and on June 28, 1750 married Sarah Belding. When she died in 1756 he removed to Wethersfield and on November 29, 1756 married her cousin Lois Belding. He taught clockmaking to his son Joseph. He was very religious and deeply attached to his mother. His family was remarkable for longevity, the average ages of Ebenezer and his nine children who grew to maturity being over eighty-three years. He died in Wethersfield in 1808.

JOSEPH BALCH, *Wethersfield*
(B. 1760—D. 1855)

Joseph Balch, a son of Ebenezer and his second wife, was born in Wethersfield on February 16, 1760, was a drummer boy in the Revolutionary War, and later carried on the trades of clockmaking and silversmithing in Wethersfield until 1794, when he moved to

Williamstown, Massachusetts. In 1810 he removed to Johnstown, New York, and died there on December 5, 1855, having given up clockmaking about the time of his removal from Connecticut.

TIMOTHY BARNES, *Litchfield*

(B. 1749—D. 1825)

Timothy Barnes was born in Branford, April 8, 1749, a son of Timothy and Phebe Barnes. His parents moved to Litchfield soon after his birth and he spent his life in that town. He served for a few weeks in the Revolutionary War in 1776, and in 1782 he married Eunice Munson of Wallingford. His sister Lois became the mother of James and Wooster Harrison, the clockmakers, who may be assumed to have been instructed in the trade by their uncle Timothy Barnes. He was a silversmith and a maker of both brass and wood clocks. He died in Litchfield on October 11, 1825.

MILES BEACH, *Litchfield & Hartford*

(B. 1743—D. 1828)

Miles Beach was born in Goshen on November 14, 1743, a son of Adna and Hannah (Miles) Beach. Miles' father was a first cousin of Macock Ward the Wallingford clockmaker, and it is reasonable to surmise that the latter may have taught young Beach his trade. Beach followed clockmaking and silversmithing in Litchfield from about 1765 to 1785. He was a major in the Revolutionary War and a selectman in Litchfield in 1777.

In 1785 Beach in partnership with Isaac Sanford, an engraver, moved to Hartford and on June 27th advertised;

> Beach & Sanford, Having removed from Litchfield to this City, and opened a shop about ten rods south of the Bridge, Purpose to carry on Engraving, Clock and Watch Making and Mending, in all their various branches in the newest and most tasty manner.

This partnership was dissolved three years later in June, 1788, Beach continuing to carry on clockmaking and work in silver at the original shop, where, in 1790, he took his apprentice James Ward into partnership. They conducted the business together for seven years, doing a great variety of work other than clockmaking, such as making copper stills, tea kettles, iron stoves, brass trumpets, buckles, swords and saddlery hardware. They dissolved the partnership in June, 1797.

After this time Beach carried on the business alone until 1813, when he took his son John into partnership and the firm name became Miles Beach & Son.

Beach died in Hartford in 1828. He had served as chief engineer of the Hartford fire department from its organization in 1789 to 1805, was prominent in civic affairs, was one of the most skillful silversmiths of his day and undoubtedly produced many brass clock movements. His partners were probably not clockmakers, although both Sanford and Ward were versatile mechanics, the former being an engraver, miniaturist, and inventor of textile machinery and devices for making felt hats, while the latter was for many years a leading manufacturer of metal goods under the successive names of James Ward; Ward & Bartholomew; and Ward, Bartholomew & Brainard.

JOHN BENJAMIN, *Stratford*

(B. 1730—D. 1796)

John Benjamin, a son of John and Mary (Smith) Benjamin, was born in Stratford in 1730. On May 9, 1753 he married Lucretia Backus, and about that time started in business as a clockmaker, brass worker and silversmith. He was an Episcopalian and active in the affairs of Christ Church. In 1756 he acted as collector of the funds subscribed to purchase an organ for the church, and from 1758 until 1773 he served without compensation as organist. He was an ardent patriot during the Revolutionary War, holding successive commissions as captain, major and colonel, and was wounded in the battle of Ridgfield. He was town treasurer of Stratford in

1777, and served on many town committees at various dates. In his later years he owned and operated a rope walk. He died in Stratford on September 14, 1796, at the age of sixty-six.

Several examples of Benjamin's work as a silversmith are known. He is said to have made the brass weathercock which still tops the spire of Christ Church, perhaps the finest existing example of an early weathercock in America.

ZIBA BLAKSLEE, *Newtown*

(B. 1768—D. 1834)

Ziba Blakslee was born in Plymouth, Connecticut, on July 9, 1768, a son of Abner and Thankfull (Peeter) Blakslee. He removed to Newtown as a young man, took the Freeman's oath in 1791, married Mehitable Botsford of Newtown on May 3, 1792, and established himself as a clockmaker, bell founder and jeweler. In the same year he advertised in the *Farmers Journal:*

> Bell Foundry, Smithery, Jewellery &c. The Subscriber respectfully informs the public that he carries on, at his shop at the Head of the street in Newtown, the Gold-Smith's business in all its branches; casts Bells for Churches;—Makes and repairs Surveyor's Instruments;—Church Clocks and Clocks and Watches of all kinds—where orders will be punctually attended and all favors gratefully acknowledged, by the public's humble servant
>
> Newtown, March 27, 1792. Ziba Blakslee.

He continued to reside in Newtown until his death November 9, 1834, aged sixty-six. Shortly after 1820 he took his son William into partnership and the latter successfully carried on the jewelry business for many years after Ziba's death.

ABEL BREWSTER, *Canterbury*

(B. 1775—D. 1807)

Abel Brewster was born in Preston, February 6, 1775, a son of Benjamin and Elizabeth (Witter) Brewster.

In 1796, when twenty-one years old, he opened a clock and

silversmith's shop "a few rods south of the First Society Meeting House in Canterbury" and advertised that he made clocks and time-pieces of various descriptions and repaired watches. By 1797 he had begun to feel the effects of the long term credit which was customarily extended at the time, and in his advertisement of clocks, watches and silverware, he announced that "as those who trust long, cannot sell cheap long," he was under the necessity of asking for immediate settlement of all accounts more than three months outstanding. He took an apprentice to the clock and jewelry trades in 1799, and in 1800 again announced that he had different types of eight-day repeating clocks for sale as well as a long list of silverware and jewelry, and that he would be glad to exchange some of this merchandise for a saddle horse. He continued working in Canterbury until the latter part of 1800, when he moved to Norwich Landing and opened a shop. Early in 1805, however, he advertised for a successor to the business, and in April of that year, sold out to Judah Hart and Alvin Wilcox, retired, and died in 1807, age thirty-two years.

JOSEPH BULKLEY, *Fairfield*
(B. 1755—D. 1815)

Joseph Bulkley, a son of David and Sarah (Beers) Bulkley, was born May 1, 1755 at Weston, Connecticut. It is possible that he was apprenticed to John Whitear, Jr., and after the death of the latter he became the leading clockmaker of Fairfield. On July 27, 1778, he married Grizzel Thorp. They were members of Christ Church, Fairfield, where they renewed their baptismal covenants on May 30, 1779. A number of Joseph Bulkley's clocks are still running in the vicinity of Fairfield. He served in the Revolutionary War, resided in Fairfield throughout his active life, and died there June 2, 1815, at the age of sixty years. His tombstone stands in the old Fairfield burying ground. A typical example of his engraved dials is shown on Plate 20.

DANIEL BURNAP, *East Windsor & Coventry* (B. 1759—D. 1838)

Daniel Burnap was born in Coventry November 1, 1759, a son of Capt. Abraham and Susan (Wright) Burnap. He settled in East Windsor about 1780, where he carried on an active business in clockmaking. One of his first apprentices was Eli Terry, who later became the foremost clockmaker of America.

Burnap's clocks were of unusually fine workmanship. He was a skillful engraver, and his engraved brass and silvered dials were admirable. While he probably made a few wooden clocks, similar in design to those produced by the Cheneys, his fame rests upon the handsome brass eight-day clocks upon which he specialized. On March 14, 1791, he advertised,

Brass Wheel'd Clocks. The subscriber having for a number of years applied principally to the business of Clock Making, and having met with considerable encouragement in the business, takes this method to inform the publick that although he works in many other branches common to those in the silversmith line, as also Surveyor's Compasses, Watch repairing, &c., yet notwithstanding Clock Making is intended as the governing business of his shop, and is determined that no pains shall be wanting to merit the approbation of his customers. Clocks of various kinds may be had at his shop in East Windsor, on short notice on the most reasonable terms (warranted). Those persons that may be in want of public clocks may be supplied at the above shop, and may depend on a faithful performance, by the publick's humble servant,

Daniel Burnap.

N. B. Wanted as Apprentices to the above business, 2 or 3 likely active Boys, about 15 or 16 years old. Cash given for Old Brass if delivered soon.

Burnap's account book for this period is still in existence, and many of the entries relating to the clock business are of interest. He was one of the most prolific of the Connecticut craftsmen of his day and his clocks, although not particularly scarce, are considered among the most interesting and valuable of late eighteenth and early nineteenth century work. One of the finest existing examples of a Burnap clock is the eight-day musical clock which stood in his own home and is still in the possession of his descendants.

On May 18, 1795 he advertised:

> A Journeyman Cabinet-Maker, who is a workman at Clock-Case making, may meet with employment by applying to Daniel Burnap, of East Windsor, who wishes to contract for the making of 15 or 20 cases.

Shortly after 1800 Burnap moved from East Windsor to that part of Coventry now known as Andover, and in 1805 he built the homestead which he continued to occupy during the remainder of his life. He was for many years justice of the peace and held court in a spacious room on the first floor of this house. His shop, which has long since disappeared, was located a few rods east of the house. Here he continued to make clocks, silver spoons and buckles, and brass saddlery hardware, and to repair watches. In his later years, probably before 1815, he gave up this shop and the responsibility of apprentices, and fitted up a room in the attic of the house where he could keep busy at the less arduous kinds of work such as engraving and repairing watches. Here he had his work bench and tools, a regulator on the wall and a little iron stove in the center of the room. Much of his time was spent in caring for his extensive farm, but he never entirely gave up mechanical work, although he probably made few clocks after 1815.

About 1825 he broke his hip. While he recovered sufficiently from this accident to be able to walk with the aid of a cane and even to mount his horse, his activities were considerably restricted, and toward the end he used a crutch.

He was a kindly but taciturn man. It is said that one of his pleasures late in life was feeding the wild birds and protecting them from the depredations of the boys in the neighborhood. Even the quail would congregate in his farmyard for the grain which he scattered for them.

He died in 1838 at the age of seventy-eight, a prosperous and respected citizen.

JOSEPH CARPENTER, *Norwich*

(B. 1747—D. 1804)

Joseph Carpenter was born in Woodstock on July 4, 1747, a son of Joseph and Elizabeth (Lathrop) Carpenter. It is possible that he served his apprenticeship in Massachusetts, but about 1769 he moved to Norwich and established himself as a clockmaker and silversmith in a shop belonging to his stepfather Joseph Peck. He paid a yearly rental of £1/10/0 for this shop, but in 1773 he leased land from the pastor of a neighboring church and erected a shop of his own which is still standing on Norwich Town Green. In 1775 he married Eunice Fitch.

His advertising was confined to an occasional announcement that he wished to employ an apprentice at clockmaking, such announcements appearing in 1775, 1789 and 1790. When he died in 1804, William Cleveland appraised his shop as follows:

1	CHIME CLOCK MOVEMENT, FACE PARTLY DONE	30.00
1	CLOCK ENGINE	16.66
9	MOVEMENTS OF 8 DAY CLOCKS WITH WHATEVER APPERTAINS TO THE SAME, CASES EXCEPTED	90.00
1	30 HOUR MOVEMENT	7.00
5	SMALL TIME PIECES	20.00
1	ROUND FACE ANVIL	9.00
1	STAND VISE	2.50
1	SMALL VISE	1.00
1	PLATING MILL	5.00
1	TURNING LATHE	6.00
2	TURN BENCHES & BARREL TOOL	4.50
9	SPOON PUNCHES	3.00
	SHOP TIME PIECE	6.00
	ALL THE TOOLS, FINISHED AND UNFINISHED WORK AND EVERYTHING APPERTAINING TO THE SHOP LATELY IMPROVED BY THE DECEAS'D NOT BEFORE PARTICULARLY SPECIFIED IN THIS INVENTORY	30.00
3	CHERRY CLOCK CASES	30.00
1	MAHOGANY DITTO	15.00

ASAHEL CHENEY, *East Hartford & Northfield, Mass.*

(B. 1758—D.)

Asahel Cheney, eldest son of Benjamin Cheney, the clockmaker of East Hartford, was born about 1758, for although no exact record of the date of his birth has been found, John Fitch, one of Benjamin's apprentices, recorded that in 1761 Asahel was about two years old and that he was then a "smart, sensible active boy."

He followed his father's trade of clockmaking for a short time in East Hartford, moving later to Northfield, Mass., where in 1790 he was listed as a property owner and was carrying on "an extensive business in the manufacture of eight day clocks." His name appeared in Northfield records in 1797 when he was again referred to as a clockmaker, but no notice of his death has been found. An interesting example of a wood clock made by Asahel in East Hartford is shown on Plate 47.

BENJAMIN CHENEY, *East Hartford*

(B. 1725—D. 1815)

Benjamin Cheney was born in East Hartford on September 8, 1725, a son of Benjamin and Elizabeth (Long) Cheney. He was probably apprenticed to Seth Youngs of Hartford about 1739 to learn clockmaking, starting in the business on his own account in East Hartford about 1745. He made brass and wood clocks as well as various small brass articles, and trained several apprentices, among them no doubt his brother Timothy, John Fitch a pioneer inventor of the steamboat, and his own sons Asahel (who moved to Northfield, Massachusetts), Elisha (who settled in Berlin), Martin (who moved to Windsor, Vermont) and Russel (who moved to Putney, Vermont).

Fitch described him in the following words:

> My master was a pretty good sort of a man, but possessed with a great many odities and considerable deformed with the rickets in his youth, especially his head which was near double the size of common proportions

and was a man of some considerable genius. He married one Deborah Allcott in the same parish.

My mistress was as well as a very silly woman a very lazy one as well as proud and as bad a housekeeper, who had the best that the world afforded in victuals and would get drunk as often as she could come across licquor.

Altho my mistress was extravagant in some things, she was rather penurious in others, yet my master was always willing that I should have a belly full of such as was going, but it frequently happened that it was very indifferent.

Benjamin Cheany followed nothing in the shop but wooden clocks and small brass work, and my indentures was ambigously exprest that he was to learn me clockwork and brass foundering. Before this time I had found my mistake and that he was not obliged to learn me anything but Wooden Clocks which he paid no attention to but kept me almost the whole of the time that I was in the shop at trifling pottering brass work, and was when I left him almost totally ignorant of clockwork.

In 1764 Benjamin Willard moved from Boston and commenced the business of making shoe lasts at Cheney's house. On December 3, 1764, he advertised in the *Connecticut Courant* as follows:

Benjamin Willard, Last maker from Boston, Has recently set up his business at East Hartford at the House of Benjamin Cheney, where Shoe Makers and others who want Lasts, may be supplied on the most reasonable terms, either by the Set or Single One.

N.B. Said Lasts may also be had at Caleb Bull's in Hartford at the sign of the Boot and Shoe, in King-Street.

Willard was twenty-one years old at this time. His connection with Cheney, while not an apprenticeship, was such that he learned enough of clockmaking to be able to engage in that business upon his return to Massachusetts some years later. He apparently instructed his younger brother Simon in the trade, and the latter, as is well known, became by far the most noted clockmaker in Massachusetts.

By 1778 Cheney was engaged in making nails and tacks, the Revolutionary War having largely increased the demand for these items during the time when clocks could not be sold. On September 22, 1778, he advertised:

Wanted, as an apprentice to the nailing business, a healthy lad about 14 years old. Enquire of Benjamin Cheeny.

and again on May 15, 1779:

Eight & Fourteen ounce tacks, and Four Penny Nails to be Sold by—Benja. Cheney.

With the return of more settled conditions he may have resumed clockmaking, but some time before the end of the century he gave up active work and moved with his wife to Berlin to live with his son Elisha. It is said that he became greatly enfeebled in mind and body during his later years. He died in Berlin on May 15, 1815, at the age of ninety.

A fine example of Benjamin Cheney's work is shown on Plate 34. It was made for Moses Butler, probably about the year 1750 and stood in the Butler tavern on Main Street, Hartford. In 1801 it was inventoried as worth $15.00. The movement is of wood.

ELISHA CHENEY, *Berlin*

(B. 1770—D. 1847)

Elisha Cheney was born in East Hartford on January 11, 1770, a son of Benjamin Cheney, the clockmaker. He doubtless received his mechanical training from his father, and in 1793 he moved to Berlin and married Olive North, a sister of Simeon North, the pistol maker of Middletown. Elisha made both brass and wooden tall clocks, and was for a time in partnership with his brother-in-law North, making pistols. On December 19, 1800, they advertised:

Wanted, at the Pistol Manufactury at Berlin, five or six Journeymen Lock Filers to begin by the 15th of February next. Those that can come well recommended may meet with good encouragement by applying to
North & Cheney.

In 1801 Elisha bought a shop on the line between Berlin and Middletown and began turning out wooden clocks in quantities.

At first he made wooden tall clock movements but in later years produced various styles of wooden shelf clocks. About 1833 he gave up the business and moved to Illinois, where he died in 1847.

TIMOTHY CHENEY, *East Hartford*

(B. 1731—D. 1795)

Timothy Cheney, a brother of Benjamin Cheney, was born in East Hartford on May 10, 1731. He was a clockmaker, a watch repairer, blacksmith, joiner and silversmith. He made both brass and wooden clocks, having probably learned the trade from his brother. While Benjamin and Timothy Cheney are usually mentioned together, there is nothing to indicate that they were ever associated in the clock business. Both of them lived and worked in East Hartford, but as entirely independent artizans and at no time as partners.

John Fitch, who worked for Timothy for a few months after leaving Benjamin's shop, wrote of his experiences as follows:

Timothy Cheney followed making brass and wooden clocks and repaired watches, and agreed to take me for one year and learn me the three branches. I was set to work at small brass work with the exception of being shortly put to clock work and going out once in a while to work on his place and at his shop which he was building that summer, tending on masons, carpenters, &c. I was not put to one single clock, neither wood nor brass, during that time. It is true I did begin one wooden one, but never had time to finish it.

As to watch work, I never saw one put together during my apprenticeship, and when I attempted to stand by him to see him put one together, I was always ordered to my work, and what was the most singular of all, it was but seldom that I could get to see his tools for watch work, as he had a drawer where he was always particularly careful to lock them up. He never told me the different parts of a watch, and to this day I am ignorant of the names of many parts."

In 1768 Timothy was appointed a lieutenant of the 6th trainband of Hartford, and in 1769 was promoted to captain of the "Five Miles" trainband. In 1774 he was on the war committee, and in 1775 led one of the first Hartford companies of troops, but was relieved from active duty within a few weeks in order that he might devote himself to making granulating sieves for the manufacture of gunpowder.

About 1790 he built a sawmill and gristmill on the stream a mile south of what is now South Manchester Center, and near it a homestead which is still standing.

He died in East Hartford in 1795, leaving a considerable estate. His tools, which were appraised at £15-0-0, consisted of "Clock, Watch, Gold, Silver & Blacksmith, Carpenters & Joiners Tools, together with the Stock."

JOSEPH CLARK, *Danbury*

(B. —D. 1821)

Joseph Clark was working as a clockmaker in New York at least as early as 1768 when he advertised "some exceedingly good eight-day clocks in very neat mahogany cases." He soon afterwards removed to Danbury, and was living there in 1777 when he bore arms in the Danbury raid of that year. In 1787 he married Anna Stedman of Danbury, and in 1791 advertised in the *Farmers Journal:*

> Clocks and Watches. Joseph Clark, Informs his customers and others, that he continues the business of Clock and Watch Making, at his Shop in Danbury; where he makes and repairs, Chime, Repeating, Day of the month, Age of the Moon, with a second from the center, and Plain Eight-Day Clocks; Day of the Month, Skeleton and Plain Watches. He also carries on the Gold and Silversmith business in all its branches. All kinds of Plated Buckles made at said Shop.

Somewhat later in the year he announced that his shop was "near the Printing-Office in Danbury," and that "Shipping Horses, Country Produce, &c. will be received in payment for Clocks." In 1795 he was offering "a number of Eight-Day Clocks with or without cases." In 1811 he removed to New York State, and later to Alabama where he died about 1821.

WILLIAM CLEVELAND, *New London & Norwich* (B. 1770—D. 1837)

William Cleveland was born December 20, 1770, at Norwich, a son of the Rev. Aaron and Abiah (Hyde) Cleveland. He was apprenticed to Thomas Harland, and in August, 1792, at the age of twenty-one, he moved to New London and entered into partnership with John Proctor Trott under the firm name of Trott & Cleveland. They took over the shop left vacant by the death of Gurdon Tracy. Trott was a gold- and silversmith, but apparently not a clockmaker.

Trott & Cleveland advertised as clock- and watchmakers, goldsmiths and jewelers. In 1793 they bought land in New London on the street running from the courthouse to the market, but in 1794 Cleveland disposed of his share in this property to Trott, and early in 1796 the partnership was dissolved, Trott continuing as a goldsmith and employing a journeyman clockmaker to attend to that branch of the business, while Cleveland is said to have moved to Worthington, Massachusetts, and later to Salem. He remained in Massachusetts but a short time, and then returned to Norwich where he resumed clockmaking. He appraised Joseph Carpenter's clock shop in 1805 and helped to settle up the latter's estate. In 1807 he went to New York, but soon moved back to Norwich, and continued to reside there during the remainder of his life.

Upon his return to Norwich Cleveland entered the partnership of Erastus Huntington & Co., merchants, but on October 1, 1811, this concern was dissolved, Cleveland settling up the accounts and advertising in January 1812:

> Watch Repairer. The subscriber has resumed his former business of Watch and Clock repairing, making gold Neck-laces, Silver Spoons and all the variety of articles commonly connected with the business of a Watchmaker and Jeweller.

In 1812 he commenced the operation of a pottery for the manufacture of stoneware at Bean Hill, Norwich, but he sold this business to Armstrong & Wentworth in May, 1814. Like so many of his contemporaries, he had doubtless abandoned active clockmaking about the beginning of the century.

He died in 1837 at Black Rock, New York, while on a visit to his son-in-law. His grandson, Grover Cleveland, was a president of the United States.

HENRY J. COOLIDGE, *New Haven*

(B. —D.)

On August 28, 1787, Henry J. Coolidge advertised in the *New Haven Chronicle:*

Henry J. Coolidge—Begs Leave to inform the Public that he has opened a Shop, the third Building south of the Church, in Church Street: where he makes and sells Repeating, Horizontal, Seconds, Day of Month, and Plain Watches, Also Watch Repairing done in the best and neatest Manner, upon the shortest notice.—N.B. Spring, Chime, and Spring Quarter Clocks, with Moon's Age, Day of Month and Seconds, to stand on Desks or Burows, Common Eight-Day Ditto with Weights.
New Haven, Aug. 28, 1787 H. J. C.

LEWIS CURTIS, *Farmington*

(B. 1774—D. 1845)

Lewis Curtis was born in 1774, a son of Gabriel Curtis of Farmington. In 1795 he opened a clockmaker's and silversmith's shop in Farmington, having, it is said, served an apprenticeship to Burnap. His father helped to establish him in business, paying, among other things, 13 shillings to Judah Woodruff, a carpenter, to make the show window for the shop. This shop was located on Main Street about a hundred feet west of the present Elm Tree Inn. It is still standing although not on its original site.

In 1797 Curtis advertised that his shop had been broken open and various pieces of silver stolen. In 1799 he advertised:

Lewis Curtis, Respectfully informs his friends and the public at large that he still continues to carry on the Clock Making Business—such as

Chime Clocks that play a number of different tunes, and clocks that exhibit the moon's age, common eight day Clocks, and Time Pieces of various kinds—such may be had at his shop on short notice. . . .

He left Farmington in 1820, removed to St. Charles, Missouri, and subsequently went to Hazel Green, Wisconsin, where he died in 1845.

JOHN DAVIS, *Fairfield (?)*

(B. —D.)

The only clear record of John Davis which has been found is the following agreement. Perhaps he was a young apprentice of John Whitear. The Fairfield vital records show the birth of a John Davis in 1730, but the latter has not been identified as the clockmaker.

> An agreement made this 25th day of Feby. 1750-51, between the Church Wardens of Christ Church in Stratford, and John Davis, clock maker, a stranger, and is as followeth:
>
> That the said Davis is to keep the clock of said church in good repair for two years from the date hereof and to have for his labor five pounds for each year, provided the said clock goes well the said time; if not, he is to have nothing for his labor, and the first five pounds to be paid at the end of the first year, and the other five pounds at the second year; and that the Church Wardens are not to be put to more trouble about paying the money than to pay it either in Stratford or Fairfield; and to be paid in old tenor money.

WILLIAM DISTURNELL, *New Haven & Middletown*

(B. —D.)

William Disturnell "from London, Clock, Watch-maker and Jeweller &c." opened a shop on College Street, New Haven, in 1784, but in 1786, "for the benefit of his family" he removed to Middletown. He had been "recommended from London to Col. Clement Biddle, at Philadelphia; from thence to Pierpont Edwards Esq. at New Haven." His scanty advertising indicated that he specialized in making and repairing watches, and the extent of his clock-making activities is unknown.

ENOS DOOLITTLE, *Hartford*

(B. 1751—D. 1806)

Enos Doolittle was born in Wallingford on May 17, 1751. His father, whose name was also Enos, was a younger brother of Isaac Doolittle, the clockmaker of New Haven. Enos Doolittle senior died in Wallingford in 1756 when his son was only five years old. Young Enos served an apprenticeship under his uncle Isaac Doolittle in the latter's shop in New Haven and by 1772, when twenty-one years old, he had completed his apprenticeship, made his first clock, and moved to Hartford. On December 15, 1772, he ran his first advertisement in the *Connecticut Courant* announcing the establishment of a clockmaking business at the printing office.

> Clocks. All kinds of Clocks, Surveyor's & Mariner's Compasses, made clean'd and repair'd, by the Subscriber at the Printing office in Hartford. And as he has serv'd a regular apprenticeship to those Branches, with the most noted workman in this Colony, he flatters himself he will be able to supply any gentlemen that will favor him with their custom as much to their Satisfaction and on as reasonable terms as they can be supplied elsewhere, and their Favours will be greatefully acknowledged by their humble Servant, Enos Doolittle.

By April of the following year he had employed a London trained journeyman watchmaker to assist with the growing business, and in October he employed a journeyman clockmaker who occasionally helped with the repairing of watches. He bought a set of watchmakers' tools for the use of his employees, but the latter must have turned out to be somewhat less than capable and energetic workmen, for on December 5, 1774, Doolittle advertised:

> Wanted, a Journeyman Clock Maker that CAN and WILL work. Good wages will be given and punctual Payment made to such an one that will immediately enter into the service of Enos Doolittle.

On September 25, 1775, he announced:

Clocks and Watches. The subscriber begs leave to acquaint his customers in particular and the public in general that he continues making Clocks and repairing Watches in the neatest and best manner. He has for sale, crucibles, pumice-stone, and rotten stone at his shop under the printing office in Hartford. Enos Doolittle.

After this date specific mention of clockmaking ceased in his advertising, and during the Revolutionary War he apparently devoted himself largely to watch repairing. In July 1776 he was selling "four different views of the battle of Lexington and Concord, neatly engraved from original paintings taken on the spot." These were the work of his well-known contemporary and namesake, the New Haven engraver, Amos Doolittle, being impressions of the first copper-plate engravings made in America.

In 1781 Doolittle bought the homestead of Joseph Reed which had been confiscated by the state when Reed joined the British during the Revolutionary War, and a year later, in 1782, he and Barzillai Hudson acquired a part of the land on which the old printing office stood. They divided this land, about a third of an acre, into lots, on one of which Doolittle built a shop where he continued to carry on his trade.

In 1784 he was still repairing watches, and in 1785 was making brass and wooden surveyors' and mariners' compasses, selling them at his shop in Hartford and through agents in Middletown and Saybrock.

In 1786 he offered a clock and case for sale but did not indicate whether it was one of his own make. In 1787 he added a brass foundry to his other activities and advertised on October 22nd:

Enos Doolittle

Having purchased all the Stock and Tools belonging to Mr. Williamson, and employed a workman, who has been regularly bred to the Brass Founding Business, proposes making all kinds of Brass Handirons, Candlesticks, Coach, Chaise, Sleigh and Mill Work, and all other articles belonging to that business, at his shop next door, north of Messers Hudson and Goodwin's printing office, where he continues to repair Watches, make Mariners and Surveyors Compasses, &c. He has for sale a Black Smith's Bellows.

In 1788, in partnership with Jesse Goodyear of Hamden, he took up the casting of church bells.

Goodyear, who was born in 1767, had probably been an apprentice to Isaac Doolittle in the latter's New Haven bell foundry, and doubtless furnished the practical knowledge of the details of the business. Although Enos himself, prior to 1772, had been an apprentice under Isaac, the latter was not at that time making bells, and prior to the association with Goodyear, Enos Doolittle had given no indication that he was acquainted with the business. The initial announcement appeared in the *Courant* on February 11, 1788:

The subscriber informs the public, that he proposes to carry on the business of Casting Bells for Churches in Partnership with Mr. Enos Doolittle, of Hartford. Having had considerable success in that branch, and having Cast Bells (weighing 2400 lb.) equal to any imported, doubts not he can give satisfaction to those who may please to employ him. The Bells will be warranted and sold on the most reasonable terms. Apply to said

Enos Doolittle or Jesse Goodyear.

Goodyear stayed in Hartford only long enough to get the foundry into successful operation, and then returned to Hamden to handle the sales of the bells in the New Haven district, Doolittle running the foundry.

The partnership lasted for three years, but during this period Doolittle seems to have carried on the other branches of his business entirely independently of Goodyear. On March 24, 1788, he advertised:

Jack at all Trades
Bell & Brass Foundery

Bells and bell metal mortors of all sizes, Brass and polished steel Handirons, Shovel and Tongs; Candlesticks; Phaeton and Chair Harness; Brass Caps and Boxes for wheels; Door Handles and Knockers; Chiney

Hooks; Mill Brasses; Printing Presses; Paper Moulds; Mariners and Surveyors Compasses; Copper Nails; &c.

Likewise Watches repaired on easy terms by applying to

Enos Doolittle.

The firm of Doolittle & Goodyear was notably successful and attracted favorable (and no doubt well paid for) editorial comment on several occasions from both the *American Mercury* and the *Connecticut Courant.* The editor of the *Courant* wrote on December 31, 1789:

Last week was cast in this city by Messieurs Doolittle and Goodyear, a Bell for the town of Brookfield, State of Massachusetts, weighing 650 lb. A few months since these artists cast a Bell for the town of West-Springfield; both of which are allowed by good judges to be the equal of any of the size ever imported. As these gentlemen have been at considerable expense in erecting works for carrying on this branch of business and will engage to furnish Bells of any weight whatever on easier terms than they can possibly be imported, and warrant them to be good; it is not doubted those towns who wish to supply themselves with good Bells, will encourage so useful a manufacture in preference to sending their money out of the country.

In 1790 the partners cast a bell weighing 1100 pounds for the town of Portland, Massachusetts, reported to have been of exceptional quality.

On March 22, 1790, in their advertisement for the bell foundry, they announced that "those Societies who are in want of Public Clocks, are also informed that they can be furnished on reasonable terms by the subscribers, who have been regularly bred to that business."

On May 20, 1791, the partnership of Doolittle & Goodyear was dissolved, Doolittle continuing the bell business under his own name, although he had a partner named Newell in the brass foundry from October 1791 to November 1793. In 1793 he began to make up bells for stock, an indication that he must have found an excellent market for his product, and he continued actively making bells, mariners' compasses, protractors and miscellaneous brass goods until 1802, when he retired (probably due to ill health) and his son James Doolittle took over the bell business. In 1804 his wife Asenath died at the age of forty-five, and two years later, in 1806, Enos himself died, age fifty-six, and was buried in the Center Church Burying Ground at Hartford where his tombstone still stands.

While his son James continued the bell foundry, he did not undertake the other branches of his father's business. The brass foundry was taken over by Williamson, no doubt the same man from whom Doolittle had purchased it in 1787. The clock business was apparently turned over to Nathan Allyn, the Hartford watchmaker, for disposal. Allyn advertised it extensively and in 1808 seems to have sold it to Heydorn & Imlay. It comprised the most extensive set of clockmakers' tools in the state, and the new owners operated it with considerable success until 1811 when they in turn offered it for sale, and it apparently passed out of existence and with it the making of clocks in Hartford.

ISAAC DOOLITTLE, *New Haven*

(B. 1721—D. 1800)

Isaac Doolittle was born in Wallingford August 13, 1721, a son of Joseph and Elizabeth (Holt) Doolittle. He doubtless served an apprenticeship at clockmaking under Macock Ward in Wallingford, but moved to New Haven about 1742 and opened a shop on Chapel Street. On November 10, 1743, he married Sarah Todd. His business life extended over more than half a century, and he was without doubt one of the leading manufacturers and most versatile mechanics of the state during the second half of the eighteenth century. His business pursuits were by no means confined to clockmaking.

In May 1758 the General Assembly appointed him Armourer of the Fourth Regiment of Connecticut.

In 1760 he was selling imported silver watches and in 1763 he advertised "Isaac Doolittle near the college in New Haven, Has to sell, Clocks and Watches—Clock and Watch Glasses,—Bar-Iron, —Chocolate,—Surveyors' Compasses, &c." In 1764 he was serving as tax collector in New Haven for the "Proprietors of the Township of Ludlow, in the Province of New Hampshire."

On September 7, 1769, the *Boston News Letter* remarked:

> We are informed that Mr. Isaac Doolittle, Clock & Watch maker, of New Haven, has lately completed a Mahogany Printing-Press on the most approved construction, which by some good Judges in the Printing Way, is allowed to be the neatest ever made in America and equal, if not superior, to any imported from Great-Britain. This Press, we are told, is for Mr. Goddard, of Philadelphia, Printer.

In 1770 Doolittle advertised that he had employed a European trained watchmaker and that he made all sorts of clocks as well as surveyors' and mariners' compasses, and in August 1774 he advertised:

> Isaac Doolittle of New Haven, Having erected a suitable building and prepared an apparatus convenient for Bell-Founding, and having had good Success in his first attempt, intends to carry on that Business, and will supply any that please to employ him, with any Size Bell commonly used in this, or the neighboring Provinces, on reasonable Terms.

In 1775 he was one of the commissioners having charge of the erection of a beacon on Indian Hill which was to be used to give an alarm if the British should attack the town of New Haven.

In July 1776 the *Connecticut Journal* carried the following advertisement:

> The subscribers, having erected a Powder Mill near this town, would hereby inform the public that they are ready to receive any quantity of Salt Petre for manufacturing into Powder.
>
> Isaac Doolittle
> Jeremiah Atwater
>
> Who want to purchase a quantity of Sulphur, for which they will give a generous price.

This powder mill was located in Westville, and turned out large quantities of powder during the Revolutionary War.

Doolittle was active in the affairs of Trinity Church, serving as warden at various periods from 1765 to 1785 and contributing the largest single amount toward the building of the church. Shortly after 1785 his health failed and he was forced to suspend business activities for a few years, but in January 1788 he was able to announce:

This is to give notice to the Public in General and to my former Customers, that I, the subscriber, hath so far recovered my health, that I carry on the repairing of Watches, making of Clocks, Screws for Clothiers; also the Casting of Bells, and every other kind of business that used to be carried on before my late illness, at my shop in Chapel Street. All favours will be gratefully received by the Public's humble Servant,

Isaac Doolittle.

He continued making clocks and casting bells until 1797 when his health again failed, and on February 20, 1800, the *Connecticut Journal* contained the announcement:

"Died in this city, after a long and distressing illness of several years continuance, Mr. Isaac Doolittle, in the 79th year of his age; a very worthy and respectable character."

His son Isaac, Jr., succeeded to the business and no doubt took over the equipment which was inventoried as follows:

1 GLUE POT	2–6	1 MARKING IRON	0–9
1 AUGER	1–0	1 PAIR SHEARS	6–0
2 SAWS	3–0	1 BIT STOCK	3–0
1 IRON SQUARE 18″	0–9	DRILL & GOUGES	3–0
1 PAIR CUTTING PLIERS	1–0	13 NEW SMALL FILES	3–3
1 PAIR DIVIDERS	4–0	1 LARGE SCALE & IRON WEIGHTS	36–0
1 PAIR BELLOWS	1–6	1 PAIR SMALL SCALES	2–6
1 LARGE IRON LATHE	9–0	1 FRAMED SAW	1–0
2 IRON FLASKS	2–0	1 SMALL PLANE	0–9
2 COPPER FLASKS	6–0	1 SMALL VISE	5–0
1 STAKE	3–6	4¼ LBS. LEAD PATTERNS	1–8
1 ANVIL	55–0	2¼ LBS. OLD POLISHING FILES	1–10
1 BEAK	10–0	1 DOZ. OLD FILES	2–0
1 GRAVING TOOL	4–6		
4 HAMMERS	6–0		

1	TIME PIECE	6–0		SUNDRY WATCH TOOLS	15–6
1	BRASS SQUARE ENGRAVER	1–0	1	LEAD STONE	30–0
30	OLD FILES	2–6	1	SPRING TOOL	6–0
1	WIRE PLATE	1–0	1	CLOCK ENGINE	24–0
4	SCREW PLATES	6–0	1	WATCH PLATE	1–6
2	SMALL IRON LATHES	9–0	1	SET FIGURE STAMPS	3–0
2	SMALL VISES	4–0		HALF OF A WATCH ENGINE	18–0
1	PAIR CRUCIBLE TONGS AND 1 LADLE	3–0	1	SCRAPER	2–0
				SUNDRY TOOLS	10–0
1	SLEDGE	6–0	1	MAGNET	24–0
1	HAMMER	2–0	1	DIAMOND	28–0
1	BROKEN VISE	6–0	3	WATCH STAKES	3–0
2	PR. SPOON MOLDS	12–0	2	COMPASS PLATES	24–0
1	STAKE	9–0	1	PAIR SHEARS & PLYERS	3–0
1	LOGGER HEAD	3–0	1	UNFINISHED CLOCK	60–0
1	LATHE & WHEEL	12–0			

ISAAC DOOLITTLE, JR., *New Haven*
(B. 1759—D. 1821)

Isaac Doolittle, Jr., a son of Isaac the clockmaker, was born in New Haven in 1759, served an apprenticeship under his father, and on December 7, 1780, married Desire Bellamy of Cheshire, a sister of the distinguished Rev. Dr. Bellamy of Bethlehem, Connecticut. He started in business in New Haven at about this time, and on June 7, 1781, advertised in the *Connecticut Journal:*

> Compasses of all kinds, both for sea and land, surveyor's scales, and protractors, gauging rods, walking sticks, silver and plated buttons, turned upon horn; also clocks and watches made and repaired, and a variety of other work, by Isaac Doolittle, junr. at the house lately occupied by Mr. William Noyes, in Leather lane, New Haven.
>
> N.B. Said Doolittle, wants a lad of about 13 or 14 years old to serve as an apprentice to his business.

He was apparently not a particularly active clockmaker, but seems to have specialized somewhat on surveyors' and mariners' instruments. Just prior to his father's death he took over the latter's business, and on May 22, 1799, advertised:

The subscriber having commenced business at the shop lately occupied by Mr. Isaac Doolittle, in Chapel Street, where he repairs watches, makes and repairs Surveyor's Compasses and Chains, Brass Amplitude, plain brass and common Ship's Compasses, Gauging Rods, Quadrants, repair'd &c. every favor gratefully received by the public's humble servant,

Isaac Doolittle, jun.

He died in 1821.

EZRA DODGE, *New London*

(B. 1766—D. 1798)

Ezra Dodge, who was born at Pomfret in 1766, was an apprentice of Thomas Harland. He commenced business early in 1787 at a shop on the main street of New London where he made all kinds of clocks and silverware. He soon took an apprentice at clockmaking, and in April 1788 moved his shop to the location formerly occupied by John Champlin, the noted New London goldsmith. A few months later he moved again, and finally in 1790 built a shop of his own on the main street opposite Winthrop's wharf. He married Elizabeth Hempstead in 1790.

In 1798 he advertised that he had for sale a general assortment of groceries, and rum, brandy, gin, molasses and flour by the barrel, and that "He still carries on the clock and Watch making and gold and Silver Smiths business in all their branches."

He was one of the first to succumb to the epidemic of yellow fever in New London in 1798. In a contemporary account of this epidemic he was mentioned as "Ezra Dodge, watchmaker, clockmaker, gold and silversmith, brass founder, gunsmith, locksmith, grocer, &c. An ingenious mechanick, good man and valuable citizen." In spite of his varied activities his estate was insolvent.

His shop equipment, which was very complete, consisted of the following items:

1 CLOCK ENGINE	30.00	1 SMALL LATHE & WHEEL	3.50
1 WATCH ENGINE	30.00	1 LARGE PLATING MILL	30.00
1 LARGE LATHE & WHEEL	12.00	1 LARGE ANVIL	7.50

1	LATHE	3.58
1	LARGE FORGING HAMMER	1.25
1	SMALL FORGING HAMMER	.75
1	PLANISHING HAMMER	.91
1	HAND VISE	.67
1	PAIR CUTTING NIPPERS	.67
1	PAIR ROUND PLIERS	.41
1	PAIR SPRING PLIERS	.67
1	PAIR FORGING TONGS	.33
1	PAIR KNEALING TONGS	1.00
1	LARGE VISE	4.51
2	PAIR IRON FLASKS	1.75
2	WIRE PLATES	1.50
1	SAW FRAME	.50
1	SMALL HAMMER	.25
1	RIVETING HAMMER	.25
1	BEAM COMPASSES	1.00
1	MANDRIL	.75
2	DRILL STOCKS	.83
3	PAIR CHARGING TONGS	.25
1	SCREW ARBOR	.23
3	BURNISHERS	.37
7	WORN FILES	.48
1	PEAN HAMMER	.41
1	OIL STONE	2.83
3	CLOCK BROACHES	.83
1	LARGE BREAST BIT STOCK	.75
12	ENGRAVERS ARBORS &C.	1.00
	SMALL SCALES & WEIGHTS	.33
	PUNCHES & CHISELS	.41
1	SMALL BENCH VISE	1.67
2	PAIR WATCH PLIERS	.83
1	WATCH MAGNIFYING GLASS	.42
1	SCREW PLATE WITHOUT TAPS	.25
2	WATCH BRUSHES	.11
1	SCREW KEY	.25
8	WATCH FILES MOSTLY WORN	.67
3	CLOCK FILES	.25
2	BURNISHERS WITH IVORY HANDLES	.33
1	ENGRAVER WITH IVORY HANDLE	.17
18	WHIRLS & DRILLS	1.50
1	DRILL HAND	.33
1	VERGE VISE	.25
1	SMALL WATCH LATHE	1.50
1	CASE STAKE	.25
1	MAIN SPRING TOOL	1.00
1	CARVED TIME PIECE	2.00
1	BRASS TIME PIECE	12.00
1	LOT CLOCK PINIONS	.42
2	PAIR STEEL CLOCK HANDS	.18

DAVID ELLSWORTH, *Windsor*

(B. 1741—D. 1821)

David Ellsworth was born in Windsor on March 27, 1741-2, a son of David and Jemima (Leavitt) Ellsworth, and a brother of Oliver Ellsworth, Chief Justice of the United States. He was probably an apprentice to either Seth or Benjamin Youngs in Windsor, and commenced business as a clockmaker, watch repairer and dentist in Windsor about 1763. On February 22, 1779, he married Phebe Lyman of Goshen. During the Revolution he made muskets for the army. He seems to have been a general handy man and all around mechanic, occupying much the same position in Windsor that Lowrey did in Wethersfield. He died in Windsor on January 4, 1821, aged seventy-eight.

DUDLEY EMERSON, *Lyme*

(B. 1765—D.)

Dudley Emerson was born in Lyme on February 3, 1765, a son of Broadstreet and Jemima Emerson. On January 25, 1788, he advertised in the *Connecticut Gazette:*

Clock & Watch-making & Jewelry Carried on By Dudley Emerson, In Lyme, East Society, on the road from New London to East Haddam, Where he makes Chime Clocks that carry hours, minutes and seconds, day of the month and moon's age; eight day repeating ditto; thirty-hour do. and eight day time pieces. Watches repaired in the best manner, and at the shortest notice. Said Emerson having served a regular apprenticeship at the above branches, flatters himself he shall be able to give satisfaction to those who favor him with their custom. Cash given for old gold, silver, brass and copper.

N.B. Wanted a steady, well-minded Boy, about 15 or 16 years of age, as an apprentice to the above occupations, by said Emerson.
Lyme, Jan. 23d, 1788.

WILLIAM FOOTE, *Middletown & East Haddam*

(B. 1772—D.)

William Foote was born in Colchester on August 4, 1772, a son of Charles and Jerusha (Chamberlain) Foote. In June 1795 he moved to Middletown and went into partnership with Samuel Canfield, a silversmith, under the firm name of Canfield & Foote. They carried on a clockmaking and silversmithing business until July 4, 1796, when the partnership was dissolved and Foote removed to East Haddam, taking a shop near the landing opposite Col. Champion's store, where he continued for a short time to make various kinds of clocks and to work in silver. He later moved to Michigan and died there some time after 1836.

JOHN FORBES, *Hartford*

(B. —D.)

John Forbes, a "Clock and Watch Maker from Philadelphia," settled in Hartford in 1770, and on October 7th of that year advertised in the *Courant:*

> The subscriber hereby informs the public that he has set up the business of Clock and Watch Making at the shop of Mr. Stephen Austin, Taylor in Hartford—and likewise determines (if the public will favor him with their custom) to treat them in the best English manner. He hath not such a stock of arrogance as to warrant his work for three years without any manner of reserve; he intends to do his work, and that shall be his recommendation. John Forbes.

The reference to a three-year warrantee was a reply to the advertisement of Lanbier Lescoit, of Hartford, who had announced that work repaired by him would be "warranted for three years."

JAMES GRANT, *Hartford & Wethersfield*

(B. —D.)

James Grant, a London trained clock and watchmaker, settled in Hartford in the summer of 1794 and rented the shop of "Mr. William Sloan, next door to the Loan Office." He advertised to repair "Repeaters, Horizontal or common French or English Watches; Musical, Chime and common clocks." In September, 1794 he advertised in the *Hartford Gazette:*

> James Grant, Clock & Watch Maker; from London. Begs Leave to inform his friends and Customers, that have been pleased to favour him with their orders, that for their convenience and his own, he has removed his shop to Mr. Gibsons, two Doors South of the Meeting House in Main Street, Hartford. Where he continues to mend and repair all sorts of Watches as usual, on the most reasonable terms, and insured to perform for one year at least, baring accidents. In part of said Shop he means to manufacture Clocks compleat, a specimen of which he intends to lay before Judges of the same line of Business, and to public view, as soon as he can get his Shop in ample order.
>
> Hartford, Sept. 18.

He apparently received but slight encouragement in his efforts at clockmaking, for on October 19, 1795, he described himself as "James Grant, Clock and Watchmaker from London, but now Mender and Repairer."

On November 7, 1796, after two years' residence in Hartford, he announced that he had moved his shop to Dr. Bernard's house, nearly opposite the Meeting House in Wethersfield, where he would continue to repair watches and clocks.

DAVID GREENLEAF, JR., *Hartford*
(B. 1765—D. 1835)

David Greenleaf, Jr., was born in Norwich in 1765, served an apprenticeship under Harland, and in 1788 settled in Hartford where he opened a shop "eight rods north of the court house" and commenced making clocks and silverware, repairing watches, and selling jewelry. He undoubtedly made a few clocks prior to 1796, but in May of that year he announced that he found it difficult to carry on a number of lines of mechanical work and that henceforth he would confine himself entirely to watch repairing. He had business dealings with Harland up to the time of the latter's death in 1807, and it is not improbable that he sold Harland's clocks in Hartford, as he continued to advertise clocks for sale long after he gave up making them. In 1804 he entered into a partnership with Frederick Oaks under the name of Greenleaf & Oaks, Jewelers. He was a member of the Hartford Common Council in 1806 and achieved some local prominence. About 1811 he closed his store and took up the practice of dentistry. He died in Hartford in 1835.

EDWARD GRIFFITH, *Litchfield*
(B. —D.)

Edward Griffith emigrated from England, settled in Litchfield in 1790, and advertised,

Edward Griffith, Watch and Clock-maker, from London, most respectfully informs the inhabitants of Litchfield,—that he—makes plain Watches and Clocks on the most approved plan, and on reasonable terms, in the town of Litchfield.

Somewhat later in the year he advertised for two apprentices at clock- and watchmaking, but shortly afterwards removed to Savannah, Georgia, where in 1796 he was advertising as a watchmaker.

DANIEL WHITE GRISWOLD, *East Hartford*
(B. 1767—D. 1844)

Daniel White Griswold was born in East Hartford on March 26, 1767, a son of White and Elizabeth (Cheney) Griswold. He was a nephew of Benjamin and Timothy Cheney, the clockmakers; was apprenticed to Timothy Cheney about 1782, and was working on his own account as a clockmaker in East Hartford about 1788, but probably gave up the trade before 1800.

At least four of his tall clocks fitted with wooden movements and engraved brass dials are still running in the vicinity of East Hartford. His principal business was that of a trader between New York and Boston. He owned a small powder mill on the stream near Union Village, but sold this to Hazard, Loomis & Brothers, the powder monopolists of New England, about 1830. He died December 27, 1844.

BENJAMIN HANKS, *Mansfield & Litchfield*
(B. 1755—D. 1824)

Benjamin Hanks was born in Mansfield on October 29, 1755, a son of Uriah & Irene (Case) Hanks. He was a skillful and energetic mechanic who made clocks, carried on a goldsmith business, was a maker of stockings, looms, compasses, brass cannons, and large church bells. He advertised from Windham on May 16, 1777:

Benjamin Hanks, Clock & Watch Maker, opposite the Court House, Windham, Takes this method to inform the Public that he makes and has for sale, chiming, repeating and common eight day Clocks;—Watches made and repaired on the shortest notice; He likewise keeps a Workman in the Stocking Weaving Business, at his shop in said Windham, where constant Attendance is given and the smallest Favours greatfully acknowledged. Those favoring him with their Custom in the weaving Business, are desired to spin their yarn fine. Cash given for fine Thread and Worsted.

Although but twenty-two years old at this time, he was exercising his ingenuity to improve stocking machinery, and on August 14, 1777, he presented the following interesting petition to the General Assembly:

To the Honorable General Assembly of the State of Connecticut, now sitting at Hartford within said State. The Representation and Memorial of Benjamin Hanks of Windham in said State to Your Honors humbly showeth that he relying upon a Belief that Your Honors are ever desirous to promote & Encourage every useful manufactury within this State, he hath taken encouragement to address your Honors upon the Subject of fabricating Stocking Looms; to perform and Effect which he conceives that he is sufficiently skilled, that he your memorialist has been much used to and acquainted with laboring in Iron, Brass, and Steel and every other material necessary to construct the proposed machine; that he is fully persuaded that he could with some small Encouragement, soon construct and finish a number of such Looms to the satisfaction of the publick and every skillful Weaver therein; that he conceives that having compleated his desires in that particular, that the publick would be greatly Benefited thereby, not only in more readily and cheaply supplying the Soldiery with that necessary part of Clothing, viz. Stockings, but also the Inhabitants of the State; but your Memorialist being young, and not of sufficient cash to procure those materials which are necessary for the desired purpose, he is thereby unable and prevented from making the Attempt; Whereupon he humbly prays your Honors to take the matter into your just consideration and grant to him such Premium as your Honors may think proper upon his having compleated a good and sufficient Stocking Loom, and upon such other conditions as are fit and suitable; and in the meantime intrust him (upon proper Security) with a Sum sufficient for the purpose; or otherwise grant him such encouragement as to your Honors may seem meet. And he as in Duty bound shall ever pray. Dated in Windham this 14th day of Aug. 1777. Benjamin Hanks.

This petition was denied, and whether Hanks proceeded with his plans for "fabricating stocking looms" is unknown. He did, however, continue to make clocks, and on April 1, 1779, advertised:

Benjamin Hanks, Clock and Watchmaker in Windham, Returns Thanks to his Friends and Customers for their kind Encouragement in the above Trade; and begs leave to inform the public in general, that he still continues to carry on said Business in all its various Branches. He also has workmen in the Gold and Silversmith Business, which make and have for Sale, Gold Beads, and Buckles of all kinds of the newest Fashions, also plated Spurrs, Spring Lancets, &c. Those that incline to employ him in his said Branch of Business, may depend on having their Work well done, and the Favors suitably acknowledged, by their humble servant,

Benj. Hanks.

In 1780 Hanks moved from Windham to Litchfield, and built the homestead which is still standing and is now numbered 82 South Street. He shortly afterwards took a contract to make a clock for the Old Dutch Church at Nassau and Liberty Streets, New York City, and in 1783 he petitioned the General Assembly for a patent on a clock to be automatically wound by air. This patent was granted, reading as follows:

Upon the petition of Benjamin Hanks of Litchfield showing to this Assembly that he has with great study for a number of years applied himself in search of mechanical knowledge, and in pursuance thereof has invented and executed a clock which winds itself up by the effect of air, and which will continue so to do without any other assistance till the component Parts thereof are destroyed by Friction, and that said clock will keep time in the most regular manner as it is wound up without any variation or stop put to its mechanical operation, and that consequently said invention is a great improvement in mechanical knowledge and praying for the privilege of an exclusive Right to make and Vend Clocks so constructed for the Term of fourteen years as by memorial on File—Resolved by this Assembly that the Prayer of the said Petition be granted.

In 1785 he advertised:

Benja. Hanks, Clock and Watch-Maker, in Litchfield, Presents Thanks to his Customers for the Encouragement and Patronage, with which he has been favoured, in the above Branches;—and begs leave to inform them and the Public in general, that he still makes and warrants Horizontal Watches, shewing seconds from the Centre, and Day of the Month—Skeleton and Eight-day Watches in gilt and plain Silver Cases—Eight-day chiming, repeating and Pneumatick Clocks, in Mahogany and Cherry-tree Cases—Also, Church Clocks that will go without winding—Surveyors Compasses—The gold and Silversmiths Business—engraves Seals with Cyphers and Coats of Arms.

In 1786 he began casting church bells in Litchfield, and on August 19, 1787, the *Fairfield Gazette* contained the following item:

Litchfield, August 6. The ingenius Mr. Hanks, of this town, to whom the public are indebted for that curious piece of mechanism, the invention of air Clocks, on Saturday last placed an excellent Bell in the belfry of our meeting house, which he cast at the expence of the society (the old one being broken). It is well rought, and sounds very grateful. We do not communicate this advice as anything wonderful or prodigious—We only announce the success of the artist, with a view that he may be encouraged by others, particularly in this county; as he has been at considerable trouble and cost in constructing his Foundery.

Bells, to the church the living call,
And to the grave they summons all.

We could wish the gentlemen of the Town of Fairfield, and its vicinity, might be stimulated with the same laudable sentiments as those of Litchfield—and furnish our New Fabrick with a Bell, as the expense would be but trifling to the Society.

Early in 1790 he announced that "the Brazier's Business will be carried on (for a few weeks only) at the shop of Mr. Benjamin Hanks, a few rods south of the Court House," and shortly afterwards he removed to Mansfield, where he continued to make clocks and bells and carried on a woolen business.

In 1808 he took his son Truman into partnership in the bell business and started another foundry in Troy, New York, advertising on July 20, 1808:

Bells Cast in the old foundry at Mansfield, Conn. and at Troy, N. Y. by Benjamin Hanks & Son. They also have surveyors compasses upon the

Rittenhouse improved plan. The business will be managed in Mansfield by Truman Hanks of Ashford.

On November 4, 1816, Hanks was granted a patent for "Moulding and Casting Bells." He was then living in Albany but spent a part of his time in Mansfield overseeing the business in that place. He died in Troy in 1824, leaving a farm of 100 acres "where the said Hanks resided while in Mansfield," and a quarter interest in a woolen mill in the same town. The bell business in Troy passed into the hands of the Meneelys and is still in successful operation.

THOMAS HARLAND, *Norwich*

(B. 1735—D. 1807)

Thomas Harland was born in 1735 in England. He learned the trade of clock and watchmaking in that center of the art, traveled on the continent of Europe, and due no doubt to the depressed condition of the clockmaking trade in England at the time, emigrated to the American Colonies in 1773. It is said that he came from England in one of the ships which carried the tea destroyed at the Boston Tea Party and that it had been his intention to settle in Boston, but that the prevailing excitement in that town caused him to change his plans. Be that as it may, he went at once to Norwich, where he established a clock shop. He had brought his tools from England, and on December 9, 1773, he inserted the following advertisement in the *Norwich Packet:*

Thomas Harland, Watch and Clock-maker from London, Begs leave to acquaint the public that he has opened a shop near the store of Christopher Leffingwell, in Norwich where he makes in the neatest manner and on the most approved principles, horizontal, repeating and plain watches in gold, silver, metal or covered cases. Spring, musical and plain clocks; church clocks; regulators, &c. He also cleans and repairs watches and clocks with the greatest care and dispatch, and upon reasonable terms.

N.B. Clock faces engraved and finished for the trade. Watch wheels and fuzees of all sorts and dimensions, cut and finished upon the shortest notice, neat as in London, and at the same price.

During his first winter in Norwich, Harland boarded with Samuel Leffingwell and made a clock for him which is illustrated on Plate 44. One of his early customers was the patriot Nathan Hale, who, while on a visit to Norwich to see his sweetheart, employed Harland to repair a watch.

In November 1774 Harland thanked his patrons for their encouragement in the trade of clock- and watch-making and announced that he was employing jewelers at his shop. He had arrived in Norwich at a time when the inhabitants of that town had but recently agreed upon a policy of non-importation of English goods and had placed imported clocks among the articles to be taboo. That Harland profited greatly by this policy seems evident and his mastery of his trade enabled him in a short time to build up a very substantial business.

In 1778 he purchased a plot of land from David Nevins, and having married Hannah Clark in 1779, he built a homestead in which he lived throughout the remainder of his life. The house, greatly altered, is still standing.

On April 13, 1787, he advertised:

Clocks & Watches

The Subscriber has left with him for Sale, a few very neat gold and silver Watches; made by some of the best Workmen in London; which he will sell at a very small Advance from the London Price, for good Pay.

He has also for Sale

a variety of Watches and clocks of his own making, shewing Seconds, day of Month, Skeleton and Plain; with chain, spring, eight-day and thirty-hour clocks.—Also a small assortment of Jewelry, plated good, Chains, Seals, &c. for Cash or Produce, on the lowest Terms.

Watches clean'd and repair'd as usual on the shortest notice.

Wanted

a sober, diligent Boy; about 14 years of age, as an Apprentice to the above Trades. Thomas Harland

Norwich, April 10, 1787.

In 1788 he superintended the construction of a fire engine for the town. Upon its successful completion, an attempt was made by one Samuel Thomas, a coachmaker who had constructed some of the parts of the engine, to claim sole credit for "this piece of curious workmanship." To this attempt, Harland replied in the *Norwich Packet:*

The gentlemen of Norwich Landing having determined to purchase a Fire Engine—expressed a wish that I would inspect some of the latest made and most approved machines of that kind, and if there were any new improvements I might adopt them.—Having found one that appeared to me superior to any I had seen, I took the exact plan and dimensions of it, and as I did not see anything I could make improvements upon, I adhered to said plan with very little intentional variation. Mr. Samuel Thomas assisted in making said engine; he did all the wood-work, and also assisted in some other parts of the machinery. The valves, the pistons, the large screws for the several joints, I made myself; two of my apprentices, with a smith, and a founder were also employed occasionally, till the whole was compleated.—I never entertained an idea that it could be considered as a proof of mechanical genius to construct a machine so simple, so frequently and accurately delineated, so common, and so open to inspection as the Fire Engine.

By 1790 tradition says that Harland was employing as many as ten or twelve apprentices engaged in turning out clocks, watches and silverware, and that his annual production amounted to forty clocks and 200 watches.

On May 15, 1794, he advertised in the *Packet:*

The Subscriber has for sale at his shop in Norwich Bailey's new invented and much approved

Patent Steam Jack's

executed under the direction of Joseph Pearsall in New York.

This machine is exceedingly well calculated for general use, as it may be moved to any fire-place, will carry any reasonable weight, and so simple in its construction as to be very little liable to injury or decay. Said Subscriber has also for sale, Watches and Clocks of most of the various kinds in use, also, Gold Beads, Buckles, Spoons, Ear-Rings &c. Cheap for Cash, Produce or on Short Credit.

Cash and the highest price given for old Gold, Silver, Copper or Brass.
Norwich May 15, 1794 Thomas Harland

N.B. A Boy of about 13 or 14 years of age, of a steady and industrious turn, wanted as an Apprentice.

In December 1795 his shop was destroyed by fire. The *Norwich Packet* described the fire as follows:

Between the hours of 11 and 12 on Friday evening last, the valuable clock and watch manufactury belonging to Mr. Thomas Harland of this city, was discovered to be on fire; the destructive element was raging with such fury before it was discovered as to render all exertions for preserving any part of the building totally abortive. Attempts were made to get out some of the most valuable articles but it was found wholly impracticable to save any thing whatever.—the building had a small insurance upon it; but the loss at a low valuation is computed at 1500 dollars! through the calmness of the night and the spirited exertions of the citizens the flames were prevented from communicating to any of the adjoining buildings.

Although sixty years old at this time, Harland immediately re-established his shop in a building belonging to David Nevins. In 1800 he advertised "chime spring & plain eight day clocks with enamel'd and silver'd faces, completely finished and regulated, in mahogany and cherry cases," and "American Watches." On February 10, 1802, his advertisement in the *Norwich Courier* read:

The Subscriber Has for sale, at his shop in Norwich, an assortment of new Warranted Watches,—viz.—English silver Watches, cap'd and jewelled; Day of Month, and seconds, in silver and gilt cases; second hand do. various sorts; French Gold & Silver Watches, day of month, second, and plain.

Clocks of various kinds, completely finished and regulated, consisting of chime, spring and plain eight day repeating, in mahogany and cherry-tree cases. Gold Beads, silver table spoons, Desert, Coffee & Tea Spoons, Sugar Tongs, Salt Dishes &c.

Surveyors' Compasses, with agate centre needles; chains and Protractors—main springs, dial plates, fuzee-chains, pinion-wire, &c. &c.

He also employs an experienced workman in the manufactory of Tin, and has on hand, a compleat assortment of Tin Wares, made of the best materials, and warranted as good and as cheap as can be purchased in the state.

A small assortment of Pewter & Japanned Ware.

Any of the above articles will be sold for cash, most kinds of country produce, tow-cloth, chek'd or white flannel, or a reasonable credit, as low as they can be procured elsewhere.

Watches repaired and warranted to perform well, on the shortest notice and most reasonable terms.

Cash given for Old Gold, Silver, Brass and Pewter—All sorts of Tin-Ware repaired. Thomas Harland

When Harland died in 1807, the *Connecticut Gazette* contained the announcement:

Died at Norwich, Mr. Thomas Harland, aged 72, Goldsmith; he is said to have made the first watch ever manufactured in America.

The inventory of his tools, dated May 25, 1807, comprised the following items:

2	WATCH ENGINES	25.00
1	CLOCK ENGINE	15.00
4	LARGE VISES	8.00
2	LARGE LATHES	8.00
1	FOOT LATHE	5.00
1	SMALL HAND LATHE	4.00
2	SETS WATCH TOOLS	30.00
2	NEW FILES	.40
2	STEELYARDS	1.25
3	OILSTONES	1.50
1	BOX SCREW & WIRE PLATES	4.00
1	PAIR PLATE ROLLERS	6.00
1	FUZEE ENGINE	5.00
1	SET CASE TOOLS	10.00
1	SMALL ANVIL	2.00
6	SMALL VISES	10.00
3	SCREW AUGERS	1.50
1	SET SCALES & WEIGHTS	.50
1	LARGE ANVIL	20.00
1	LARGE BELLOWS	3.00
	TOOLS FOR TIN PLATE WORKING	60.00
1	SET SPOON PUNCHES	5.00
	TOOLS FOR CASTING	10.00
1	CASE MATHEMATICAL INSTRUMENTS	1.25
1	DIAMOND SET IN HANDLE FOR CUTTING GLASS	1.00
	CUMMING ON CLOCK WORK	1.00
1	EIGHT DAY CLOCK	40.00
1	DITTO WITHOUT CASE	25.00
1	EIGHT DAY TIME PIECE	25.00
1	MAHOGANY CASE	15.00
3	INCOMPLETE CLOCKS	15.00

Harland was one of the most important single figures in the history of early Connecticut clockmaking. He was a well-educated and very skillful mechanic, his clocks were superior in workmanship and were made in larger numbers than those of any of his contemporaries, but his greatest influence was in the number of apprentices trained in his shop. Daniel Burnap was the best known of his workmen, but William Cleveland, Seril and Ezra Dodge, David Greenleaf, Nathaniel Shipman, Gurdon Tracy, Benjamin Hanks, and numerous others were also trained by him. Contrary to tradition, Eli Terry was not a Harland apprentice.

JAMES HARRISON, *Waterbury*

(B. 1767—D.)

James Harrison was born in Litchfield on July 23, 1767, a son of Lemuel and Lois (Barnes) Harrison. He was a nephew of Timothy Barnes, the clockmaker, and presumably learned the trade from the latter. His account books were examined in 1858 by Henry Bronson, who noted in *The History of Waterbury*, that his first clock was sold to Major Morris on January 1, 1791, for £3/12/0, the second to Rev. Mark Leavenworth on February 2, 1791, for £4/0/0 and the third to Capt. Samuel Judd on February 19, 1791, for £4/0/0. These were probably brass clocks with enameled dials, a type of clock which Harrison made and examples of which survive. He was doubtless working on Southington at this period, for he advertised from that town on February 9, 1795, as follows:

> James Harrison, Respectfully informs his friends and the Public at large, that he carries on the business of Clock Making, which are made of brass, steel and wood (the principle part however is of wood) in the neatest manner and warranted. Gentlemen who will please to favor him with their custom may be supplied on short notice and cheap for cash.

Later in the year 1795 he removed to Waterbury and opened a shop which tradition says was in the lower room of a schoolhouse. Here he made clocks; shoe heels; reels, flyers and spools for spinning wheels; and carried on a general joinery business.

About 1800 he removed to a little shop seven feet by nine feet in dimensions located on the south side of North Main Street on the Little Brook where he installed a water wheel said to have been the first to be used in Waterbury for driving machinery. On April 15,

1802, he leased this shop for a term of seven years. He is reputed to have brought the first piano into Waterbury. He was an ingenious mechanic but a poor business man and his clock business soon passed into other hands. He left Waterbury about 1810 and was living in Boston in 1814 when he was granted a patent on an improvement in wooden clocks. He later returned to Waterbury and worked, probably as an employee, in a shop on Grand Street which belonged to his nephew, but he eventually went to New York and died there in poverty.

WOOSTER HARRISON, *Trumbull & Newfield*
(B. 1772—D.)

Wooster Harrison, a son of Lemuel and Lois Harrison and a brother of James Harrison, the clockmaker, was born in Litchfield on June 18, 1772. He settled in Trumbull about 1795 and engaged in clockmaking. On June 18, 1800, he advertised in the *American Telegraphe:*

> Wooster Harrison
> Clock-maker
>
> Respectfully informs his Friends, and the Public, that he has removed from Trumbull to Newfield; and has commenced his business over the Store of Sherman & Wheeler—where his kind of Clocks may be had on short notice.—he has employed a good workman for the purpose of repairing Watches.

HEZEKIAH HOTCHKISS, *New Haven*
(B. 1729—D. 1761)

Hezekiah Hotchkiss was born in New Haven in 1729, the eldest son of Caleb and Ruth (Munson) Hotchkiss. He learned the trade of clockmaking at an early age and by 1748, when only nineteen years old, had a shop of his own in New Haven, was known as a clockmaker and was engaged in turning out various small metal articles in addition to an occasional clock. For several years he and his brother John (a Yale graduate) were in partnership as dealers in European and West Indian goods, but this partnership was dissolved in August 1755, and Hezekiah then seems to have devoted himself entirely to his mechanical work.

He was a typical Yankee Jack-of-all-trades, including those of blacksmithing and dentistry, and combined clockmaking with a varied hardware business. He made buckles, buttons, pewter spoons, nails, and scales and sold tools such as joiners' bits and files. His equipment was extensive for that time and his stock of goods was substantial.

Hotchkiss died in 1761, from the effects of an inoculation for smallpox, when only thirty-two years old. The inventory of his tools follows, some of the items doubtless being stock which he had for sale rather than equipment for his own use. The full list is given, not because the tools were all necessary for clockmaking, but in order to visualize one of the largest establishments of its kind in that day and because it is one of the earliest Connecticut clockmaking inventories of which we have record.

Qty	Item	Value
1	GRINDSTONE & IRON AXEL-TREE	4–0
1	PAIR OF SMALL SCALES & WEIGHTS	1–6
4	ROUND FILES	1–8
10	NAIL CUTTERS	15–9
7	PAIR OF HORSE SHOE PINCHERS	12–3
68	LARGE FLAT FILES	1–14–4
22	HALF ROUND FILES	8–3
9	FLAT FILES	4–6
5	SMOOTH FLAT FILES	2–0
4	HALF ROUND FILES	2–0
1	BENCH VISE	9–4
11	DIVIDERS	9–9
26	BITS FOR JOINERS & COOPERS	9–6
18	SMALL POLISHING STONES	1–2
2	PAIR OF COOPERS COMPASSES	10–6
1	PAIR OF BRASS SCALES	9–9
3	TURNING ARBORS	1–0
1	PAIR OF SCALES	4–6
1	MANDRIL	1–0
1	PAIR OF PINCHERS	0–9
2	PAIR OF BLACKSMITHS TONGS	2–0
3	SCREWDRIVERS	1–0
2	SCRAPERS	1–0
1	PAIR OF RIVETING STOCKS	1–0
1	NEW AX	6–0
1	BOX WITH A LARGE NUMBER OF PATTERNS	12–0
1	BOTTOM STAKE & HORSE	11–3
1	PAIR LARGE SHEARS	10–0
1	PAIR LARGE BELLOWS	2–5–0

2	PAIR OF FLASKS	6–6
4	PAIR OF BUTTON MOLDS	11–6
1	SMALL ANVIL	6–0
2	DOZ. FILE HANDLES	1–0
108	SMALL FILES	1–3–7
1	JOINERS RULE	1–6
1	SET INSTRUMENTS FOR PULLING TEETH	2–10–6
1	SET OF PUNCHES TO CUT BUCKLES	3–0
76	FILES PARTLY WORN	1–17–0
36	SMALL FILES	9–0
17	PAIR OF SCALES	1–11–10
2	PAIR OF SPOON MOLDS	9–0
1	BLOW PIPE	2–0
1	GRAVING TOOL	10–0
1	GIMLET	1–0
2	SCREW ARBORS	1–0
1	CLOCK CASE	2–0–0
2	PARTLY MADE CLOCKS	8–10–0
1	TURNING LATHE	15–0
1	PAIR OF SLIDING TONGS	2–0
1	BOW SAW	1–3
3	CLOCK HAND PATTERNS	1–0
1	BEAM COMPASS	2–0
2	LARGE HAMMERS	3–6
3	SMALL HAMMERS	2–3
1	NAIL HAMMER	1–0
2	GOLDSMITHS HAMMERS	2–6
4	SMALL HAMMERS	1–4
1	ENGINE	2–15–0
1	VISE	15–0
1	OLD VISE	8–0
3	HAND VISES	3–0
1	OIL STONE	3–0
6	PAIRS OF PLYERS	4–0
2	PAIR OF SCREW PLATES & TAPS	6–0
2	PAIR OF HAND SHEARS	3–0
10	COLLETS	3–4
15	LBS. OF OLD FILES	5–0
2	HOLLOW PUNCHES	4–0
1	GOUGE	0–6
2	BURNISHERS	1–0
1	PIKE GIMLET	0–6
1	SQUARE	1–0
1	SHOP & LAND WHERON IT STANDS	30–0–0

NATHAN HOWELL, *New Haven*

(B. 1740—D. 1784)

Nathan Howell, son of Stephen Howell, Jr., was born in New Haven on January 1, 1740/41. On November 13, 1766, he married Susanna Munson, who died December 15, 1770, age twenty-five, and on January 14, 1778, he married Anna Cook, who survived him. He died December, 1784, age forty-four.

His shop was completely equipped for making brass clocks except for the absence of a wheel cutting engine. In connection with his tools, the fact that he had an unfinished clock in process of construction at the time of his death is persuasive evidence that he was a true clockmaker. The absence of the wheel cutting engine from his inventory can be accounted for either on the assumption that it was overlooked by the appraisers, or that it had been disposed of prior to the date of the inventory. One of his clocks is owned by the New Haven Colony Historical Society.

The following inventory of Nathan Howell's tools was made February 21, 1785:

Item	Value	Item	Value
1 LARGE SCREW VISE	1–0–0	1 BLOW PIPE	1–6
1 SMALLER SCREW VISE	6–0	1 PAIR LARGE SHEARS	14–0
1 LATHE	12–0	1 SCRAPER	1–0
1 SMALL LATHE	5–0	5 HAMMERS	7–0
1 HAND VISE	3–0	1 IRON STAKE (19 LBS.)	13–2
1 POLISH VISE	5–0	1 PAIR BRASS FLASKS	6–0
1 PAIR SLIDING TONGS	2–0	1 PAIR SMALL DITTO	3–0
1 LARGE SCREW PLATE & TAPS	12–0	1 WHIMBLE	4–0
1 SMALL SCREW PLATE & TAPS	3–0	1 BROACH	1–6
2 LARGE COARSE FILES & HANDLES	2–8	1 PAIR DIVIDERS	3–0
2 SMALL FINE FILES	3–0	1 SMALL STAKE	4–0
1 LARGE FINE FILES & HANDLES	2–6	SUNDRY PATTERNS TO BUCKLES	6–0
2 SMALL ROUND COARSE FILES	1–0	1 PR. LARGE BELLOWS	2–0–0
1 DOZEN SMALL FILES	3–0	1 ANVIL	18–0
1 FROSTING TOOL	4–0	1 PR. FORGING TONGS	1–6
1 PAIR PLIERS	2–0	1 PR. CASTING TONGS	2–0
1 PAIR SHEARS	2–0	1 CLOCK BEGUN	18–0
1 BORAX BOX	1–8	SHOP	100–0–0
DRILLS, GRAVERS, PUNCHES &C.	6–0		

GURDON HUNTINGTON, *Windham*

(B. 1763—D. 1804)

Gurdon Huntington was born in Windham on April 30, 1763, a son of Hezekiah and Submit (Murdock) Huntington. On June 11, 1784, when twenty-one years old, he advertised in the *Connecticut Gazette:*

Gurdon Huntington, Informs the Public that he carries on the Clock and Watch Business in its various Branches, a few Rods North of Maj. Ebenezer Backus's Store in Windham.

In October 1789 he removed to Walpole, New Hampshire, became postmaster of that town and died there July 26, 1804. His estate, which was insolvent, was administered by Asa Sibley, the clockmaker.

SIMEON JOCELIN, *New Haven*
(B. 1746—D. 1823)

Simeon Jocelin was born in New Haven October 22, 1746, a son of Nathaniel and Ann (Wade) Jocelin. He was probably apprenticed to Isaac Doolittle to learn clockmaking. His first advertisement seems to have appeared in 1771, although he was probably engaged in the business of clockmaking as early as 1768. His advertisement on January 4, 1771, in the *Connecticut Journal* read:

> Clocks of all kinds, made in the best Manner & warranted, by the Subscriber in New Haven; who undertakes the repairing of all Sorts of Clocks, however damaged they may be, in such Manner that he will engage they shall traverse equal to any the best of Clocks.
>
> Who also repairs Watches, with Care and Dispatch. Also that he makes and sells the best Sort hard Metal Buttons, suitable for Leather Breeches.
>
> Old Brass and Pewter taken in, and the usual Price given, by
>
> Simeon Jocelin.

Early in 1773 he asked for immediate payment of outstanding accounts as he intended to leave New Haven, but he returned within a short time and continued to make and repair clocks and clean watches, and in October 1776 advertised that his shop, which had been closed during the preceding few weeks, was again open and that he was working "at clocks and watches as usual."

During the Revolutionary War and for some years afterwards, the demand for clocks was extremely limited, and Jocelin turned to other pursuits. In 1778 he was making salt and had also taken up the manufacture of watch crystals. On August 12, 1778, he advertised:

Good Home-made Salt to be sold for cash or Country Produce, by Simeon Jocelin, in New Haven—Who will give Two Thirds of a Dollar per Pound for broken Flint Glass, such as Beakers &c. in order for making Watch Crystals. Pieces less than a Crown Piece or Dollar will not do, nor those that are thicker than thin Window glass, as thick glass is very hardly blown into shape; they must be very clear and free from Streaks &c. and delivered soon. Simeon Jocelin.

On November 18, 1778, he advertised again:

Watch Glasses made and sold wholesale and retail, by the subscriber in New Haven; who will give one dollar a pound for the sides of broken beakers, or the side of large flint phials, such as are thin and very clear, and free from streaks or scratches. Also will give half a dollar per pound for the best English crown glass that is thin and clear, such as clock and picture glass. He hopes those that have any broken glass answering the above description will be kind enough to send it to Simeon Jocelin.

In 1782 Jocelin and Amos Doolittle, the engraver, published a book of church music entitled "The Choristers Companion." The plates for this work were engraved by Doolittle, and the volume was apparently well received, as Jocelin continued to sell it for a number of years and in 1790 published a second edition. A year later he published another collection of sacred music.

He probably resumed active clockmaking before 1790. Like many of his contemporaries, he did little advertising during the succeeding ten years, although in 1797 he announced that he was selling cider and currant wine at his shop.

On March 8, 1800, a patent was granted to him for a "Silent Moving Time Piece" and in October of that year he advertised as follows:

Clock Manufactury

The Subscriber intending to carry on the Clock making Business more extensively than heretofore, and being unwilling to go upon uncertainties, respectfully solicits encouragement by subscription. Those who are in want of his Clocks or Timepieces, and subscribe accordingly, shall be supplied at ten percent below the retailing prices provided twenty are subscribed for within three months after date. Subscriptions will be taken at public houses, in this and most of the adjacent towns, & by the subscriber.

The retailing prices are as follows, viz.

	Dolls.
EIGHT DAY CLOCK WITH JAPANN'D MOON FACE	45
DITTO, DITTO, PLAIN-FACE	40
EIGHT DAY TIME PIECE	20
THIRTY-TWO DAY (PATENT) SILENT MOVING TIME-KEEPER	30
EIGHT-DAY (DITTO) SILENT MOVING CLOCK WITH MOON-FACE	50
DITTO (DITTO) DITTO, PLAIN-FACE	45

The above described, to be well finished, with elegant faces, without cases, and warranted, and those not equal to expectations, subscribers will not be holden to take.

Steeple Clocks, House Spring Clocks, and Chamber Time-pieces of various descriptions, will be made according to orders and warranted.

Wanted, a good Boy, for the Clockmaking and Watch-mending business, 13 or 14 years old, from the country.

The Silent Moving Time-keeper, on trial of six months fully answers expectation; when its principles are generally known, no other recommendation will be necessary. Simeon Jocelin.

In a later description of his patented clock Jocelin remarked that it "moves on different principles from other time pieces, with fewer wheels & pinions, with less friction, and with not more than a sixth part of the usual weight, as a five pound weight is sufficient for thirty-two days, the pendulum weighing four pounds and vibrating three inches at the ball."

These patented clocks were made in both tall case and shelf models, the latter being described as "convenient as a chamber or chimney Piece," and priced at forty-five dollars when neatly cased in mahogany.

The business prospered, and in 1804 Jocelin advertised for "a journeyman clockmaker who is a complete and expert workman at brass wheel clocks." There is a tradition that in his later years he imported most of his tools and materials for clockmaking, using English castings and pinions. He made banjo clocks of the Willard type and continued actively in business up to the time of his death.

On July 13, 1809, he patented an improved pruning shear and commenced its manufacture upon a modest scale.

His knowledge of mathematics was unusual and the breadth of his cultural interests was in marked contrast to the corresponding attainments of a majority of the clockmakers of the period. His son Nathaniel became one of the leading artists of Connecticut.

Jocelin's shop tools were carefully inventoried in 1823. They make a list of several hundred items and show him to have been provided with an elaborate and up-to-date equipment for clock-making, watch repairing and work in the jewelry trades. The presence of a "framing and pitching tool" is interesting as being the first mention of this valuable instrument which occurs in Connecticut.

Jocelin died in New Haven on June 5, 1823, at the age of seventy-seven:

DANIEL KELLOGG, *Hebron*
(B. 1766—D. 1855)

Daniel Kellogg, a son of Rev. Ebenezer and his wife Hannah (Wright) Kellogg, was born in Vernon on June 25, 1766. He served an apprenticeship under Daniel Burnap in East Windsor, and about 1787 commenced business on his own account in Hebron as a goldsmith and clockmaker. On December 31, 1794, he married Susanna Griggs. From 1808 to 1810 he served as town clerk, but in 1811 removed to Colchester and in 1814 was engaged in the cotton business. In 1833 he moved to Hartford and died there February 20, 1855, at the age of eighty-eight. His clockmaking activities were apparently confined to the period prior to 1800.

ELISHA KENNEDY, *Middletown*
(B. 1766—D.   )

Elisha Kennedy was born in Norwich on May 9, 1766, a son of Benjamin and Olive Kennedy. When twenty-two years of age he moved to Middletown, opened a shop and on August 4, 1788, advertised in the *Middlesex Gazette:*

Elisha Kennedy, Begs leave to inform the Public That he intends working at the Clock and Watchmaking and Repairing, in its various Branches, in Middletown, in the Shop formerly occupied by Mr. Samuel Canfield, and now by Mr. William Johonnot.

LANBIER LESCOIET, *Hartford*

(B. —D.)

Lanbier Lescoiet was an itinerant watch- and clock-maker who worked in Hartford for less than two years. His story is completed by the following three advertisements from the *Connecticut Courant:*

May 22, 1769.

Lanbier Lescoit

Watch and Clock maker from Paris, has lately set up his business at the shop of Mr. James Tiley, Goldsmith in King-Street, Hartford, where he makes and mends Repeating, Horizontal and Plain Watches and Clocks of all kinds, in the neatest manner, and on the most reasonable Terms, and they will be warranted for three years, by their Humble Servant, Lanbier Lescoiet.

December 4, 1769

Lanbier Lescoiet
(Clock and Watch maker from Paris)
at the Sign of the Clock in King-Street,
Hartford,

Hereby informs the Public that he has removed from the Shop of Mr. James Tiley, to one opposite the Store of Messieurs Lathrop & Smith, where he continues to make and mend Repeating and Plain Watches, of all kinds, on the most reasonable terms.

Any watch that he shall mend, which shall not go true he will rectify Gratis.

September 17, 1770

Lanbier Lescoiet

Intending for London in about three weeks, desires all persons who have any demands against him to come and receive their pay and all Indebted to him are desired to make payment by that time. All who have watches in his hands are desired to come and receive them by the above time.

DAVID LOWREY, *Newington*

(B. 1740—D. 1819)

David Lowrey was born in West Hartford on July 13, 1740, a son of Thomas and Ann Lowrey, and died in Newington December 7, 1819, aged 80 years. It is possible that he served an apprenticeship under Ebenezer Balch. In 1771 he married Lucy Cole. He was a blacksmith and clockmaker in Newington throughout his active life. When the Wethersfield town clock was installed in 1791 Lowrey was chosen to inspect and approve it. During the Revolutionary War he made gun locks, and in the intervals of shoeing horses, forging hardware and making clocks, he seems to have pulled teeth for the inhabitants of Newington. A number of his clocks are in existence, such creditable pieces of work that some of his descendants have doubted that they were the product of a "blacksmith," not realizing perhaps that he, like most of the early craftsmen, was a very skillful mechanic, trained as a clockmaker but practicing those branches of mechanical trade for which there was a demand in the vicinity of his shop. At his death his "tools and iron in the Blacksmith Shop" were appraised at $86.14 but no detailed inventory of the equipment was made. He apparently never advertised his work in the newspapers, although on December 19, 1810, he advertised that an apprentice boy eighteen years old named John Barnes had run away.

SILAS MERRIMAN, *New Haven*

(B. 1734—D. 1805)

Silas Merriman was born in Wallingford on January 3, 1734, a son of John and Jemima (Wilcoxson) Merriman. He was probably apprenticed to Macock Ward. In 1760 he married Hannah Upson of Wallingford, and about that time established his home and clock shop on State Street, New Haven. He was a silversmith as well as a maker of brass clocks, and trained his two sons Marcus and Samuel in the former trade. He carried on his mechanical business up to the time of his last illness, and died in New Haven May 8, 1805, age seventy-one years.

Simeon Jocelin appraised his shop equipment as follows:

Item	Value	Item	Value
1 VISE	9–0	1 SMALL VISE	4–6
1 BOX SCREWS & TAP	3–0	1 BOX FILES & OTHER SMALL TOOLS	1–1–0
1 BOX CLOCK PATTERNS	4–0	1 BOX 2 SAW FRAMES, SQUARE & OTHER TOOLS	15–0
1 BOX SUNDRY OLD TOOLS	6–0	1 BOX OIL STONES &C.	0–9
1 BOX PARTS OF A NEW CLOCK	1–10–0	1 CORD MACHINE	3–0
1 BOX SMALL TOOLS &C.	12–0	1 TURNING LATHE	3–0
1 BENCH LATHE	3–0	1 OLD SAW	0–9
1 BLOW PIPE	0–9	1 EIGHT DAY CLOCK	12–0–0
2 SMALL TIN-CASED CLOCK WEIGHTS	2–8	1 DITTO, MOON, WITHOUT WEIGHTS	12–12–0
3 TIME PIECES	3–3–0	1 HYDROSTATIC BALANCE	6–9
2 HAMMERS	3–0		
2 PAIR FLASKS	11–3		

RICHARDSON MINOR, *Stratford*

(B. 1736—D. 1797)

Richardson Minor, a son of Rev. Richardson and his wife Elizabeth (Munson) Minor, was born at Stratford on March 5, 1736. About 1758 he commenced work as a goldsmith and clockmaker. On January 23, 1764, he married Tabitha Curtis, and died in Stratford in 1797.

COMFORT STARR MYGATT, *Danbury*

(B. 1763—D. 1823)

Comfort Starr Mygatt was born August 23, 1763, in Danbury, a son of Eli and Abigail (Starr) Mygatt. He established himself as a clockmaker and silversmith in Danbury about 1783. He was elected a member of the General Assembly in 1800 and 1802. In 1804 he advertised for one or two boys as apprentices to the clock- and watchmaking trade. On June 10, 1807, he left Danbury with his family and moved to Ohio, where he died in Canfield on October 17, 1823.

ABEL PARMELE, *New Haven & Branford*
(B. 1703—D.)

Abel Parmele, a son of Job and Betty (Edwards) Parmele, was born in Guilford on May 20, 1703. He married first in 1729 Sarah Doolittle of New Haven and settled in the latter town. In 1731 he married a second wife, Mary Beecher, and within a few years seems to have removed to Branford. He was apparently an ambitious and not wholly unimportant figure in the early industrial life of New Haven County.

In 1736 he presented the following petition to the General Assembly:

The Memorial of Abel Permele of Newhaven Humbly Sheweth That whereas your memorialist has been att great Expense of both time and money in order to gain the art and Skill of Casting Larg Bells for the use of Churches, Schools &c and hath made such Experiments as that your memorialist is well assured that he can perform to good Exeptence and much for the publick advantage of the government, Considering; 1: Your memorialist can perform the work cheaper alowing the Discount of our Currancy with that of Great Brittain than it can be brought from forrain parts. 2: The Best and principle product of our Land will scarce at any Rate make Returns. 3: A great part of the materials of which such large bells are made are the product of our Counterey and almost wholly useless for any other service. 4: If a bell shall Happen to be Split (as many are) the ReCasting again here will save the Great Expense of transportation the Resque of ye Sea &c. and now yr memorialist begs Leave to Remind this Honourable assembly that the performance is such as hath nott been attempted by any as yett in the Contery and the Charge and Expense of Such an undertaking so great and calling to mind How Ready Yr. Honours have been Duly to Incourage Such undertakings and your unwillingness that any suffer thereby and yr. memorialist being Desirous of Reaping the benifit of his own Study & Industry Humbly Requests of this Honoured Assembly that He may have the whole profit off and management of sd. afair of making and Vending Large Bells within this Collony of Connecticut for the Space of twenty years next coming, and that for the term aforsd no other person without the Liscence of yr. memorialist shall within this Collone presume to Sett up or make any Bell of a Larger size than 10 Inches Diameter or for some Shorter term or Some other way as you in yr great wisdom think best to Encourage your Humble Memorialist and yr. memorialist shall as in Duty Bound &c.

Newhaven October 19: 1736 Abel Parmele.

This petition was denied by both the upper and lower houses of the Assembly.

The following promissory note was found some years ago in the Hartford Court Records:

Branford, Feb. 13, 1741/2

I the subscriber dou promis to pay unto John Carouthers or his order the sume of therty pounds four shellings courant money or a good eight day repetting clock to be delivered at or before the tenth day of June next for value recd. this day in hand. Abel Parmele.

Clocks by Abel Parmele are still in existence. The date of his death is unknown; but he was living in 1766 at the time of the death of his second wife.

EBENEZER PARMELE, *Guilford*

(B. 1690—D. 1777)

Ebenezer Parmele was born in Guilford on November 22, 1690, a son of Isaac and Elizabeth (Hyland) Parmele. His father was a carpenter and cabinet-maker, and Ebenezer himself carried on similar lines of work in conjunction with clockmaking, boat building and the operation of a cargo sloop in which he transported merchandise up and down Long Island Sound. He was apparently the first clockmaker in the Colony of Connecticut.

On July 29, 1718, at the age of twenty-seven years, he married Ann Crittenden of Guilford, and on July 29, 1719, purchased from his parents the homestead which had been built for his maternal grandfather, George Hyland. In the deed Ebenezer's occupation was noted as "boat builder." This homestead, which he continued to occupy throughout the remainder of his life, is still standing.

On December 15, 1719, and again on December 22, 1724, he was chosen collector of the Society rate, and later served for many years as town treasurer of Guilford. He was a prominent and respected citizen, a man of substantial means and of varied attainments.

On December 20, 1726, the members of the Guilford church voted that permission be "granted to any of the Inhabitants of this parish to st up & fix a suitable Clock in the meeting house." This clock was purchased by voluntary contributions, was made and installed by Parmele, and at a town meeting held December 15, 1741, it was "Voted that for as much as Ebenezer Parmele is at considerable trouble in Rectifieing & keeping the Clock in order which is set up in the Steeple of the first Society in this Town which is beneficial to the Inhabitants, he shall be freed from Serving in any Town office so long as he continues to take care of sd. Clock." Unquestionably this Guilford clock was the first steeple clock set up in Connecticut, but it was not, as has frequently been asserted, the first in New England. What is believed to be the original clock is now preserved in the Henry Whitfield State Historical Museum in Guilford. It is an extraordinarily well built piece of mechanism of hand wrought and cast metal throughout except for the winding barrels and hand which are of wood, and its maker was unquestionably a thoroughly trained and skillful clockmaker.

On Dec. 12, 1742, a town meeting in Milford authorized the selectmen of that community to purchase from Ebenezer Parmele "ye clock which is now standing in ye meeting house and if they can purchase ye same at a reasonable rate, Then to pay for ye same out of ye Towns Treasury." The terms must have been satisfactory to the selectmen, for the clock was secured and on Dec. 9, 1745, the sexton of Milford was chosen "to take care of ye bell and clock."

On December 15, 1741, at a town meeting in Guilford, it was "upon motion of Mr. Ebenezer Parmele voted & granted that sd. Parmele or any other person may build a convenient Wharff at the Common Landing place at Sluce Creek at his own Cost which wharff shall be for ye use of the Inhabitants of this Town for their conveniency in Lading & unlading Vessells and no particular mans property." Presumably Ebenezer was at this time engaged in active trade on the Sound. On March 21, 1761, he gave to his son Ebenezer, Jr., "the quarter part of a slupe called the Aliane with one quarter of hir Loding—£213/6/0."

On April 1, 1772, he made his will, died in Guilford on September 27, 1777, at the age of eighty-seven, and was buried in the old First Church burying ground.

No inventory of Ebenezer's personal estate was filed, although in 1790, after the death of his widow Ann, their son presented an inventory of his real estate, showing that Ebenezer had owned "The Dwelling House £70, the Barn £5, Old Shop 55/, and ware house 60/". In the settlement of the widow's estate, however, an inventory of her household possessions showed that she still had a "Large Vise, Hand do., Great Steelyards and Tools for Chair Making," undoubtedly the remnants of Ebenezer's shop tools. No examples of domestic clocks made by Parmele have been found.

TIMOTHY PECK, *Litchfield*
(B. 1765—D. 1818)

Timothy Peck was born in Litchfield on August 26, 1765, a son of Timothy and Sarah (Plumb) Peck. He was connected by marriage with Miles Beach, and was possibly apprenticed to the latter, although of this there is no definite proof. He started work in Middletown about 1787 in a shop under the printing office but in 1791 returned to Litchfield, his shop in Middletown being taken over by Antipas Woodward, a silversmith. In Litchfield Peck had a shop in a brick building directly south of the court house where he made and repaired clocks and silverware. He was later interested in a sawmill and was a partner in the papermaking enterprise of Aaron Smith & Co. In 1808 this business was reorganized as Horton & Peck. Timothy died in 1818, having given up clockmaking many years before that time.

LEVI PITKIN, *East Hartford*
(B. 1774—D. 1854)

Levi Pitkin, the youngest son of Joshua and Anna (Stanley) Pitkin, was born in East Hartford on November 26, 1774. He was a jeweler, silversmith and clockmaker who prior to 1800 made a number of clocks which are still running in the vicinity of East Hartford. He was a clever mechanic and a member of the well-known family of pioneer Connecticut manufacturers.

Some time after 1800 he removed to New York State and was living in Rochester in 1828 when he was granted a patent on a beer pump. He ultimately moved to Ogdensburg to live with his son Nathan, and died in that town on June 1, 1854.

SAMUEL POST, JR., *New London*
(B. 1760—D. 1794)

Samuel Post, Jr., was born in Norwich May 16, 1760, a son of Samuel and Susannah (Grant) Post.

In 1783 he advertised:

Samuel Post, jun. Informs the Public that he carries on the Clock and Watch Business at his Shop near Mr. Miner's Tavern, where he makes new warranted Watches, and Clocks of different kinds, such as repeating, exhibiting the Moon's Age, Day of the Month, and Seconds; plain eight day and common thirty-hour Clocks; desk and hanging Time-Pieces in neat mahogany Cases, a very ornamental Mode upon a new Construction, that keeps very true Time.

N.B. Gold-smith's and Jewelier's Work of all Kinds, done at said Shop. New London, Sept. 3, 1783.

In 1785 or shortly afterwards he gave up clockmaking, moved

to Philadelphia, and opened a shop for manufacturing metal buttons. His equipment for this work consisted of two plating mills, five button moulds, three vises and five button lathes. In 1794 he had 1800 gross of metal buttons in stock.

He died in 1794 while on a visit to New Haven, and his widow, Mary, settled there after his death. His father and an illegitimate daughter known as Lucy Post were mentioned in his will as living in Norwich.

PHINEAS PRATT, *Saybrook*
(B. 1747—D. 1813)

Phineas Pratt, a son of Azariah and Agnis (Bebe) Pratt, was born at Saybrook on June 27, 1747. He was a clockmaker by trade, starting in the business in Saybrook about 1768. He served in the Revolutionary War, and was for many years a deacon of the Second Church of Saybrook. He worked with David Bushnell, the inventor of the American Turtle (one of the earliest torpedo boats) upon the construction of that craft and personally made at least one successful trip in the machine. Late in life he assisted his son Abel in building machinery for making ivory combs, a business in which the latter was a pioneer at Deep River. Phineas died on February 4, 1813, age sixty-six.

ISAAC REED, *Stamford*
(B. 1746—D.)

Isaac Reed, a son of William and Rachel (Kellogg) Reed, was born in New Canaan on December 21, 1746. He married Elizabeth Lockwood and had a family of three children. He probably commenced clockmaking in Stamford about 1768 and was working there at the trade in 1776. He was a Tory and moved to Shelburne, Nova Scotia, to escape the Revolutionary War, but returned to Stamford in 1790. In that year he joined the Methodist Episcopal Church, and Methodist meetings were held at his home for a number of years. He was a master of the Stamford lodge of Masons. He died in Stamford, probably soon after 1808.

GIDEON ROBERTS, *Bristol*
(B. 1749—D. 1813)

Gideon Roberts was born in Bristol on March 5, 1749. He was a son of Elias Roberts, one of the "First Forty Settlers" sent to the Wyoming Valley by the Sesquehanna Company of Hartford in 1769, who was killed in the battle of Wyoming on July 3, 1778. Gideon himself fought in the Revolutionary War and was imprisoned for a time on one of the British prison ships. After the war he settled in Bristol, married Falla Hopkins of Farmington, and commenced making wooden clocks in a shop near his house on Fall Mountain. He peddled his clocks as far south as Pennsylvania, where he joined the Society of Friends and adopted their dress and manner of speech.

From whom he learned clockmaking is unknown. He was probably the pioneer clockmaker of the town which later was to become the most important center of the trade in the country. His business at first was small, but it increased to such an extent that by 1812 he is said to have had as many as four hundred movements in process of manufacture at one time. His work was popular, particularly in later years in the south, and he became comparatively well-to-do.

He died of typhoid fever on June 20, 1813, during an epidemic, leaving the following clockmaking tools:

1 WHEEL CUTTING MACHINE	3.00	1 HATCHET	.34
3 LATHES	6.75	3 HAMMERS	.32
2 VISES	8.50	1 BIT STOCK	.25
1 HAND VISE	1.50	2 PAIRS CUTTING PLIERS	.65
1 OLD VISE	.50	1 MARBLE STONE TO GRIND PAINT	3.00
2 HAND SAW & TENANT	2.51	TURNING CHISELS & GOUGES	2.50
1 SCREW PLATE	.25		
1 RIVET HEADER-	.12	2 PAIR FLAT PLIERS	.40

I JOINTER	.50	I PAIR SMALL FLAT PLIERS	.16
I FLY PLANE	.25	I SHAVING KNIFE	.25
I SMALL PLANE	.25	2 TWO-FOOT RULES	.50
I SMALL GAGE	.12	I SHEARS TO CUT WIRE	.25
SET OF SMALL TOOLS FOR PUTTING CLOCKS TOGETHER	2.00	2 OLD LATHES & APPARATUS	2.50
		I SHOE HAMMER	.12

JOHN RICH, *Bristol*
(B. 1763—D. 1812)

John Rich, a son of William and Mary Rich of Bristol, was born November 14, 1763. He was one of Bristol's first clockmakers, sharing this honor with Gideon Roberts. He made wood clocks and sold watches. In the later years of his life he turned out substantial numbers of clock movements, having one hundred in process of construction when he died in 1812. His equipment was inventoried as follows:

I AUGER	.25	CHERRY TIMBER FOR CLOCK WHEELS	20.00
I STEEL SQUARE	1.50	100 FT. CLOCK FACE TIMBER	1.34
SMALL TOOLS	9.13	TIMBER FOR PINIONS	18.00
MOLDS AND SQUARE	4.25	100 CLOCK FACES	40.00
2 VISES	14.00	210 PARTS OF PARTS FOR CLOCKS	367.50
5 LATHES	15.00	7 CLOCKS	21.00
I PINION MACHINE	6.00	15 UNFINISHED CLOCKS	58.50
SHEARS AND STAKE	2.00		
I WHEEL MACHINE	12.00		

SAMUEL ROCKWELL, *Middletown*
(B. 1722—D. 1773)

Samuel Rockwell was born in Middletown on October 13, 1722, a son of Joseph and Susanna (Yeomans) Rockwell. He probably served his apprenticeship in Providence, and worked there for some years, as clocks bearing his name and that address are in existence. Prior to 1762 he had returned to Middletown, and on January 20, 1763, he married Abigail (Goodwin) Johnson, the widow of Daniel Johnson of Middletown. In addition to making clocks, Rockwell was a trader who sold coffee, sugar and molasses in the New York markets. He owned a sailing sloop of sixty tons burden and an interest in a dwelling house in the southern part of Middletown. His furniture, plate and books were those of a man of taste, but he died insolvent in 1773. His clockmaking tools were as follows:

Item	Value
1 IRON LADLE	2–0
1 8 DAY CLOCK	6–0–0
1 DITTO	6–0–0
3 CLOCKS PARTLY FINISHED	3–0–0
1 BRASS ENGINE PARTLY FINISHED	4–0
6 OLD HAMMERS	6–0
1 IRON STAKE	6–0
1 SCREW PLATE	2–6
1 BENCH VISE	18–0
1 PAIR BENCH SHARES	2–0
1 LONG IRON LATHE	3–0
1 SMALL BRASS LATHE	4–0
2 SMALL VISES	8–0
2 SCRAPERS	1–6
2 SAWS	1–0
4 COMPASSES	4–0
1 WIMBLE BIT & 6 BROACHES	5–0
4 ARBORS	2–0
1 OILSTONE	1–6
25 FILES	10–0
1 BOX WATCH TOOLS	14–0
1 SMITH'S LARGE BELLOWS	1–0–0
1 CLOCK ENGINE, 1 GROOVING TOOL, FLASKS, & SUNDRY OLD CLOCK TOOLS	3–10–0
1 GRIND STONE	6–0

HARVEY SADD, *New Hartford*

(B. 1776—D. 1840)

Harvey Sadd was born October 5, 1776, in East Windsor, a son of Dr. Thomas and Delight (Warner) Sadd. He moved to New Hartford in 1798 and advertised that he was "carrying on the clockmaking business of different kinds as may suit the purchaser, at the North end of New Hartford. Likewise the Gold and Silversmith business in all its branches."

In 1801 he married Lydia Merrill and moved to Hartford, where he advertised as a gold and silversmith, and in May 1802 he was working at the shop of Miles Beach as a plater. His name appeared in Beach's advertisements until August 1803. It is said that he later engaged in the foundry business, casting stoves, kettles and the like. In 1829 he moved to Austinburgh, Ohio, where he died October 11, 1840.

JACOB SARGEANT, *Mansfield & Hartford*

(B. 1761—D. 1843)

Jacob Sargeant was born in Mansfield on February 28, 1761, a son of Samuel and Hannah (Baldwin) Sargeant. He was married to Olive Payne of Canterbury on January 30, 1785, shortly after having started in business as a clockmaker in Mansfield.

His first advertisement in the *Connecticut Gazette* for June 11, 1784, reads:

Jacob Sargeant, Watch and Clock-Maker, wishes to inform the Public that he carries on Watch and Clock Work in all its various Branches at his Shop South of the Meeting-house, Mansfield, where he makes on the most reasonable terms, different kinds of Clocks, such as chiming, repeating, plain, eight-day, exhibiting the Moon's Age, Day of the Month and Seconds; Also, Desk eight-day time Pieces in neat Mahogany Cases, upon a good construction for keeping Time; Also new warranted Watches, made in the neatest and best Manner. Watches of all kinds repaired with carefulness and dispatch by said Sargeant.

N.B. Goldsmith's and Jeweller's Work of all kinds carried on at said Shop.

Sargeant seems to have moved to Springfield, Massachusetts, about the year 1787, where he continued in the clock and jewelry business and employed his younger brother Thomas as an apprentice. In 1795 he moved to Hartford and advertised in the *Courant* for October 26, 1795:

Clocks & Watches. Jacob Sargeant Clock and Watch-maker Informs the Public that he has established his business at the Sign of the Golden Watch, a few rods south of the State house, in Hartford, where he makes, on the most reasonable terms, all kinds of Clocks, with enameled faces of the most elegant fashion; such as chime clocks that play a number of different tunes, clocks that exhibit the moon's age, repeating and alarm clocks, and plain eight-day clocks, with various other time pieces; makes warranted silver Watches, in the neatest and best manner, and also repairs them with the utmost care and dispatch. He also carries on the Goldsmiths business—&c. &c.

Sargeant continued to advertise frequently, and became, in time, the leading jeweler and silversmith of Hartford. He, however, soon ceased to advertise as a clockmaker, but apparently devoted himself to silversmiths' work and to running a jewelry store where he repaired clocks and watches and sold them at retail.

Thus on November 28, 1796, he stated that he had received a number of warranted eight-day brass clocks which were for sale. Again on May 8, 1797, he had a long list of merchandise for sale including a number of clocks, his announcement stating that most of the articles were imported direct from London and Bristol. On May 5, 1800, and again on July 13, 1801, he was advertising imported watches and eight-day clocks, and on August 30, 1802, he announced that he had "just received and offers for sale at the Sign of the Golden Watch, on the corner south of the State House, Hartford - - chime and common eight day clocks." On November 9, 1803, he "removed his business to his new store a few rods north of the state house" and had for sale, in addition to an extensive stock of jewelry and silverware, "Eight day clocks in handsome Cases, Clock Faces, Glasses, Pinions, Bells, Balls and Capitals." In 1813 he was selling Willard's "elegant patent Time Pieces." The dials of many of the imported clocks which he sold were marked with his name, but very few actual examples of his own work are known.

He was a pompous and self-important dandy, and was one of the last men in Hartford to wear the old fashioned knee breeches and silk stockings. He died in Hartford in 1843.

NATHANIEL SHIPMAN, *Norwich*

(B. 1764—D. 1853)

Nathaniel Shipman, a son of Nathaniel and Elizabeth (Leffingwell) Shipman, was born at Norwich on May 17, 1764. He was apprenticed to Thomas Harland, and about 1785 established his own business as a clockmaker and silversmith in Norwich. Silver bearing his name is in existence and a number of his clocks are still running. The latter bear a marked resemblance to those of his master, and it is probable that a close friendship and some measure of business cooperation existed between the two men. It is said that the elms which still flourish in front of Harland's homestead were planted by Shipman, and after the death of the older man, it was Shipman who settled his estate.

On September 10, 1790, the *Norwich Packet* contained the following brief advertisement:

> Cash given for old Gold & Silver by Nathaniel Shipman, who has for sale Clocks, Watches and a general assortment of Gold-Smiths Work.

On October 11, 1794, he married Abigail Coit by whom he had two children, Lydia who grew up to be a pious spinster, and Thomas who became a clergyman.

Before the end of the century it is probable that Shipman gave up his mechanical trades. He conducted a farm and invested largely in the West Indian trade. For many years he was a Judge of the county court, represented the town of Norwich in the state legislature, and acted as moderator of town meetings. He was a somewhat formal man in social life, very precise and upright in business affairs, and was frequently called upon to settle estates and handle other commissions of trust and responsibility for his fellow townsmen. He was a very large man, weighing in his later years over 250 pounds. He died in Norwich on July 14, 1853.

ASA SIBLEY, *Woodstock*

(B. 1764—D. 1829)

Asa Sibley, a son of Col. Timothy and his wife Anne (Waite) Sibley, was born March 29, 1764, in the town of Sutton, Massachusetts. He apparently served an apprenticeship under Peregrine White in Woodstock. He settled in that place, carrying on clockmaking and work in silver and, on January 10, 1787, married Irene Carpenter of Woodstock, a second cousin of Joseph Carpenter, the Norwich clockmaker. In 1795 Asa was a member of the school committee of Woodstock.

Toward the last of the century he removed with his family to Walpole, New Hampshire, where he was chosen a selectman in 1802 and town moderator in 1807 and 1808. He later removed to Rochester, New York, and died there February 25, 1829.

NOBLE SPENCER, *Wallingford & Stratford*
(B. —D.)

The first notice of Noble Spencer which has been found is his advertisement in the *Middlesex Gazette* on April 1, 1796:

> Watches repaired in the best manner by Noble Spencer, Clock and Watchmaker, lately from London, at his shop in Wallingford. Any commands in that line left at Mr. Timothy Canfield's in Middletown, will be punctually executed and returned there.

Later in the year he removed to Stratford and on January 11, 1797, advertised in the *American Telegraphe:*

> Noble Spencer, Clock and Watch Maker Late from London Wishes to inform the public that he has taken a shop a few rods south of the Church in Stratford, where he purposes to carry on the business of making and repairing Clocks and Watches, and Gold-Smith and Jeweling business in all its branches.
>
> He wants to purchase Old Gold, Silver, Brass and Copper.
>
> Stratford, Jan. 5, 1797.

ELI TERRY, *East Windsor & Plymouth*
(B. 1772—D. 1852)

Eli Terry, a son of Samuel and Huldah Terry, was born April 13, 1772, at East Windsor. He served an apprenticeship under Daniel Burnap in East Windsor and probably received brief instruction from Timothy Cheney of East Hartford in the making of wooden clocks. Contrary to the statements made in all modern histories of clockmaking, Terry was not an apprentice of Thomas Harland. That legend is of comparatively recent origin.

Upon the termination of his apprenticeship in 1792, Terry established himself in East Windsor as a clockmaker and repairer of watches. His first clocks were fitted with silvered brass dials engraved for him by Burnap, and movements of brass or wood according to the requirements of his customers. About 1794 he moved to Plymouth and continued the business in a small way. In 1797 he was granted a patent on an equation clock, the first patent for a clock mechanism granted by the United States Patent Office, and on June 9, 1800, he advertised:

Equation Clocks. The subscriber respectfully informs the public that he has invented an improvement in clocks and Time Keepers. For the exclusive right of making and vending of which he has obtained Letters Patent signed by the President of the United States. Said improvement consists in showing the apparent together with the mean time and the difference between each; having two minute hands, turning on the same center. One of which being of a different color and pattern (that it may be distinguished) shows the mean or true time, the same as common clocks; the other together with the striking part and hour hand shows the apparent time, as divided by the sun according to the table of the variation of the sun and clock for each day in the year. The said improvement diminishes from, more than it adds to the friction of the clock, and it is not more liable to disorder than common clocks. One of said clocks is ready for sale, other clocks made and watches repaired as usual.

Plymouth (Con.) June 2, 1800 Eli Terry.

Shortly after 1800 he began to turn out wooden clocks in quantities, installing a small water power to run a saw. In 1808 he commenced work on an order for four thousand wooden clock movements and for many years thereafter he was occupied upon the large scale manufacture of cheap clocks. About 1815 he designed the thirty-hour wooden shelf clock of which hundreds of thousands were produced. He was granted a number of patents, all of which were promptly infringed upon by his competitors. He occupied a significant place in the early development of interchangeable manufacturing and became one of the outstanding New England mechanics of the first half of the nineteenth century.

From 1808 to about 1833 Terry's energies were devoted to turning out standardized wooden clocks and to the accumulation of a fortune, but about the latter date, satisfied with the material success which he had achieved, he gave up quantity manufacturing, and during the remainder of his life devoted his attention to the individual construction of a few high class special clocks and to the development of original clock mechanisms.

His son Henry described his activities during this period as follows. "He did not make clocks by the hundred, nor even by the dozen, for many years before his death, and still he never abandoned the workshop. He was during many years engaged in making now and then a church clock, a few watch regulators, and the like. The church clocks were made in three independent parts, or nearly so, the connection between each being such as not to be injuriously affected by the other. The time-keeping part was of the ordinary size, and moved by a separate weight. The striking part was moved by one large weight, and the dial-wheels by another, while that of the time-keeping part weighed only three or four pounds. The dial-wheels, hands or pointers, moved only once in a minute. Church clocks constructed in this way, were thus rendered as perfect time-keepers, and as little affected by wind or storm, as any house-clock or watch-regulator could be. These clocks were made with compensation pendulum rods, of his own design, and the escapement after a model of his own. During these years of comparative leisure, his time was mostly spent in making this description of clocks, chiefly in reference to accuracy as time-keepers, making a variety of regulators with new forms of escapements and compensation rods. No year elapsed up to the time of his last sickness, without some new design in clock work, specimens of which are now abundant. He died the last of February, 1852."

Eli Terry was thus not only the first of the clock manufacturers, but also one of the last of the craftsmen, and his shop equipment has not only the sentimental and historical interest which attaches to his name, but it represents one of the last Connecticut clock shops in which high personal skill and pride in workmanship were combined to produce with the simplest of tools, a product worthy to be compared with the best of the eighteenth century work.

Terry's equipment was as follows:

Qty	Item	Value
1	HAND VISE	1.00
1	STAKE & HAMMER	2.50
	BRACE & BITTS	3.00
1	SHAVING KNIFE	.25
1	PANEL SAW	.50
1	BACK SAW	.75
2	HAND VISES	.67
2	BENCH VISES	4.00
1	SMALL BENCH VISE	.50
8	PAIR PLYERS	1.00
1	BEAM COMPASS	1.00
2	IRON SAW FRAMES	1.00
1	SMALL BRACE	.50
1	LOT SMALL CLOCK TOOLS	1.88
1	HAND DRILL	.50
2	PAIR COMPASSES	1.00
1	PAIR CALIPERS	.50
1	LOT CHISELS & GOUGES	.50
1	LOT REAMERS &C.	.50
1	TRY SQUARE	.25
	COLD CHISELS &C.	.25
2	SMALL HAMMERS	.50
1	WIRE GUAGE	.25
1	2 FT. RULE	.12
	OIL STONES & HONE	1.00
	COLD CHISELS	.17
2	BRASS TURNING LATHES, CHUCK DRILLS & TURNING TOOLS	20.00
1	CLOCK	.50
1	SCRAPER	.13
1	ENGINE & FIXTURES	20.00
4	DRILL STOCKS	1.00
	FILES & TOOLS	5.50
1	PAIR LARGE SHEARS	1.50
1	STAKE & STEEL SCREW DRIVER	.50
1	SET PLANES	3.00
1	UNFINISHED CLOCK WITH CASE	5.00
1	UNFINISHED CLOCK MOVEMENT	1.50
1	BALANCE CLOCK	2.00
1	CLOCK IN GARRET	1.00
1	ROTARY CLOCK MOVEMENT	.50
1	GRINDSTONE	.30
1	CASE WATCH TOOLS ENTIRE	8.00
1	LEVEL	.50
1	MAGNIFYING GLASS	1.00
3	AUGERS	1.50
1	HATCHET	.33
1	ANVIL	2.00
2	HAMMERS	.50
	FORGE TOOLS	.75
1	BELLOWS	5.00
1	GRINDSTONE	.50
1	PAIR SCALES TO WEIGH GOLD	.50
1	HONE	1.00
1	STOVE PIPE & TONGS	.50

ERASTUS TRACY, *Norwich*

(B. 1768—D. 1796)

Erastus Tracy, a brother of Gurdon Tracy, was born in Norwich in 1768. He was probably a Harland apprentice. His announcement in the *Norwich Packet* for October 15, 1790, was as follows:

> The subscriber has lately opened a Shop opposite Capt. Jabez Perkins Store at Norwich-Landing; where he carries on the Clock and Watch making, Goldsmith and Jeweller's business; those who please to favour him with their custom may depend on the strictest attention and dispatch by their humble servant, Erastus Tracy.

Within two or three years he moved to New London, but worked there at the trade for only a short time, and in 1796 died of consumption at the age of twenty-eight.

GURDON TRACY, *New London*

(B. 1767—D. 1792)

Gurdon Tracy was born in Norwich January 18, 1767, a son of Isaac and Elizabeth (Rogers) Tracy, Jr. He apparently served an apprenticeship in Norwich, probably under Harland, but moved to New London in 1787. He advertised in the *Connecticut Gazette* on February 11, 1787,

> Gurdon Tracy, takes this method to inform his customers and others, that he continues to carry on the Watch and Clock making business at his shop in New-London, where all kinds of Goldsmiths and jewelry work, and plated buckles of all kinds, are made on the most reasonable terms, and shortest notice, By their humble servant, G. T.

On July 4, 1788, he advertised an extensive list of watch materials for sale and also that he continued "to carry on the Watch and Clock making, Goldsmith and Jewelry Business, in all their various branches," and again on July 3, 1789, he advertised watches and watch materials for sale.

In 1791 he bought the land on which his shop was located. Shortly before this, on December 1, 1790, he had been recommended by Thomas Harland as capable of taking care of the tower clock in the New Church in New London. Harland's letter to Melvin Wait in this connection, indicating that the older man thought well of Tracy, was as follows:

Sr. Being unwell I sent the Bearer to see what was amiss in your clock from whence he has just returned. Had the person who winds the clock known where to have applied a few drops of oyl the difficulty would have been prevented: from whence you will see the propriety of having the clock wound up by a person who is acquainted with the business. Mr. Gurdon Tracy was at my house last week and says he would be glad to wind up and take the whole care of it for a reasonable compensation. Should you see cause to give him the charge of it I have no doubt of his doing it to the satisfaction of all concerned. At the same time should any part of the work fail or give way I shall be ever ready to wait upon you at the shortest notice.

Your most obliged, humble Servant, Thomas Harland.

As a result of this letter, Tracy was given the work of taking care of the clock, his compensation being forty shillings a year, but he lived only a short time to discharge that duty. He died in New London on July 11, 1792, and was buried in the old burying ground where his tombstone is still standing.

Although but twenty-five years old when he died, he had a remarkably complete outfit of clockmaker's and silversmith's tools. One completed clock was in the shop and he was engaged upon the construction of another just before his death. In addition to his shop equipment, he had an extensive stock of jewelry and watch parts. His shop, and probably his stock and equipment were taken over by Trott & Cleveland in August 1792. The equipment consisted of the following items:

1	ANVILE 59 LB.	2–19–0
1	CAN DITTO 27 LB.	13–6
2	BOTTOM STAKES	11–0
	CHILD SPOON PUNCH	6–0
	STAKE FOR PUNCH LADLE	2–0
5	PITCHING HAMMERS	15–0
1	BOOGING HAMMER	1–6
2	SMALL PLANISHING HAMMERS	2–0
1	SMALL ROUND PUNCH	0–6
1	PAIR IRON SCREWS FOR CASTING	3–0
	LARGE VICE	18–0
	SMALLER DITTO	12–0

	SMALLEST VICE	8–0
	LARGE LATHE	60–0
	TURNBENCH	12–0
	LARGE INGOT SKILLET	6–0
	FORGING TONGS	1–6
	BEAM COMPASS	3–0
	BRACE BITT	3–0
	CLOCK ENGINE	100–0
3	SAWS	9–0
	SUNDRY DRILLS ENGRAVERS & BURNISHERS	3–0
	BLOW PIPE	3–0
4	PR. PLYERS	5–0
	MANDRILL	1–6
	DRILL STOCK & DRILLS	9–0
	WATCH TURNS	4–0
6	WATCH HAMMERS	6–0
4	CASE STAKES	3–0
2	PR. COMPASSES	1–6
2	PR. SCALES & WEIGHTS	6–0
	TURKEY OIL STONE	6–0
	RING MEASURE	2–0
	TONGS	1–6
	CLOCK	7–0–0
	PAIR LARGE BELLOWS	30–0
	WORK CASE	5–0
7	FILES	3–6
	CATGUT	1–0
7	SMALL FILES FOR WATCH-MAKING	3–6
1	TANKARD ANVILE	1–9–6
1	PORINGER DITTO 11 LB.	5–6
	SOOP SPOON PUNCH	4–6
	SWAGE FOR PORRINGER BOTTOM	1–0
	MILK POTT ANVILE	2–0
1	RAISING HAMMER	1–0
2	FORGING HAMMERS	4–0
1	RING SWAGE	1–6
1	SMALL SALT SPOON PUNCH	0–6
	LADLE &C.	2–6
	TEA SPOON PUNCH	5–0
	WIRE TONGS	5–0
	FLASK	4–0
	HOLLOW STAMP	5–0
7	HAMMERS	15–0
15	PUNCHES	6–0
	SHEERS & SUNDRY SMALL THINGS	3–0
	PLATING MILL	42–0
	WATCH ENGINE	100–0
	SUNDRY OLD FILES & HANDLES	5–0
2	HAND VICES	2–0
	PAIR SHEERS	1–0
2	PAIR CUTTING NIPPERS	3–0
	PR. SPRING PLYERS	1–0
	SQUARE & MAGNET	2–0
	TURN MACHINE	12–0
	WATCH MAIN SPRING TOOL	3–0
	WATCH PIN VICE	4–0
2	SETS BEED TOOLS	6–0
	VARIETY SMALL WATCH TOOLS	12–0
	MAGNIFYING GLASS	3–0
	WIRE PLATE	4–6
	SCREWS & PLATES	3–0
2	GRINDSTONES	7–0
1	PART FINISHED CLOCK	42–0
	DRAWBENCH	12–0
6	CLOCK GLASSES	27–0
14	POLLISHING FILES	10–6
2	PR. CLOCK HANDS	4–0
	GOLDSMITH'S SHOP & LAND	60–0–0

JONATHAN TROTT, JR., *New London*

(B. 1771—D. 1813)

Jonathan Trott, Jr., was born in Boston in 1771, a son of Jonathan and Elizabeth (Proctor) Trott. The father was a goldsmith who moved to Norwich shortly after his son was born, and later (about 1790) removed to New London. Jonathan, Jr., worked at clock-making and silversmithing in New London. In 1800 his shop was "two doors north of J. & A. Woodward's, Beach Street." In this year he advertised that he made and repaired clocks and wished to employ a journeyman clockmaker. He died in New London in 1813.

NATHANIEL WADE, *Newfield & Stratford*

(B. —D.)

Nathaniel Wade, a clock- and watchmaker by trade, removed from Norwich (where he had doubtless served an apprenticeship) to Newfield about the year 1793. He went into partnership with a man named Hall under the firm name of Hall & Wade. In 1796 they advertised:

> Hall & Wade, Sincerely thank the Public for the generous encouragement they have met with in the line of their business while in this place; they hope by their endeavours to please, to merit a continuance of the public favor. Clocks and Watches made and repaired. Gold and Silver work of all kinds done in the neatest manner.—

The partnership was dissolved within a short time and Wade moved to Stratford, where he continued as a clockmaker and silversmith until 1802, when his shop was taken over by Lyman Smith, a "Clock and Watch Maker, Silver Smith and Jeweler," while Wade himself gave up the trade and engaged in the mercantile business.

MACOCK WARD, *Wallingford*

(B. 1702—D. 1783)

Macock Ward was born in Wallingford on July 17, 1702, a son of William and Lettice (Beach) Ward. He was a lawyer as well as a versatile mechanic, and a man of considerable prominence in the community. In 1724, having completed his apprenticeship (probably under Ebenezer Parmele) he married Hannah Tyler and established a shop in Wallingford.

His name appeared on a list of Freemen of Wallingford in 1730. In 1738 he built a clock for the steeple of the Wallingford meeting house. On November 2, 1738, he was commissioned a lieutenant of the southeast company or "trainband" of Wallingford, and on October 29, 1742, was promoted to captain of the 2nd Trainband. In 1743 he served a term in the General Assembly, and on August 27, 1755, he was commissioned a captain of one of the companies of the fourth regiment raised in Connecticut to go in the expedition against Crown Point.

He is said to have owned the first pleasure carriage ever seen in Wallingford, a one-horse chaise with wheels about five feet in diameter. In 1755 he attached a mechanical device to this chaise which recorded the number of revolutions of the wheels and caused a bell to ring at the end of every mile. In addition to making clocks he at one time did an extensive business in manufacturing reeds used in hand looms, repaired watches, made buttons, clock cases (and perhaps other cabinet work) and ran a farm. His shop was attached directly to his house.

From 1766 to 1774 he served continuously as a member of the General Assembly, a position which had been filled by his father in earlier years. In 1769 the assembly appointed him a Justice of the Peace in Wallingford, and he held that office continuously by successive reappointments until 1775. He was a member of the church of England, a confirmed Tory to the day of his death, and refused to the end to sign the oath of fidelity to the State of Connecticut. No examples of his work have been found.

He died in Wallingford on May 6, 1783, leaving an estate of £435, including some thirty acres of land and a complete set of clockmakers' tools inventoried as follows:

1	CLOCK CASE	12–0
1	PIECE CLOCK WORK	3–0
1	PAIR SMALL SCALES	2–6
1	BROAD HATCHET	2–0
1	GUN STICK AUGER	1–4
1	PAIR WIRE PINCHERS	1–0
1	CLOCK WHEEL ENGINE	3–0
1	BOX SCREW & PLATES	9–0
1	SMALL GRINDSTONE	6–0
1	ENGINE FOR DRAWING WIRE	1–6
1	TAP BORER	0–6
	QUANTITY OF SMALL FILES	10–0
	A NUMBER OF PLIERS, CRUCIBLES, &C. WITH WATCH SPRINGS & SMALL TOOLS	18–0
1	COOPERS ADZ	2–6
6	GOUGES & CHISELS	1–6
	SUNDRY JOINERS TOOLS	1–0
1	LARGE VISE	15–0
	15# OLD FILES	15–0
1	PAIR BUTTON MOLDS	6–0
1	BUTTON EYE MOLD	0–4

1	TIME PIECE	30–0
1	PAIR MONEY SCALES	2–0
1	PAIR SMALL STEELYARDS	4–4
1	SCREW PLATE & SCREWS	8–0
4	WIRE PLATES	5–0
8	SLEDGES OR HAMMERS	5–0
1	PAIR OLD NIPPERS	0–6
1	LARGE GRINDSTONE	5–0
1	TINKERS ANVIL	2–0
1	SPIKE GIMBLET	0–6
1	SMALL VISE	12–0
	A NUMBER OF LATHES, HAND VISES, BREAST WIMBLES, &C.	2–0–0
3	AUGERS	5–0
1	CARPENTERS ADZ	2–0
1	SQUARE & COMPASS	2–0
1	FROW	2–0
1	JOINTER	1–6
1	PAIR OLD BELLOWS	5–0
	SHEARS FOR CUTTING BRASS	2–0
1	MARKING IRON	0–4

JAMES WATSON, *New London*
(B. —D. 1806)

James Watson, a London trained clock- and watchmaker, settled in New London in 1769 and worked for a few months as a journeyman at the shop of the goldsmith, Robert Douglass. In December 1769 he moved to John Champlin's silversmith shop near the Court House in New London and advertised that he made and repaired all kinds of clocks and watches, at the cheapest rate. From the meager information available, it seems probable that Watson was a journeyman clockmaker who worked as an employee of more enterprising men. He died in the West Indies in 1806, his residence there being accounted for by an advertisement in the *New London*

Bee of December 23, 1801, wherein Jonathan Brooks, a merchant of New London, advertised for a "journeyman goldsmith and watchmaker to work in the West Indies."

PEREGRINE WHITE, *Woodstock*

(B. 1747—D. 1834)

Peregrine White was born in Woodstock on August 13, 1747, a son of Joseph and Martha (Sawyer) White. He was a namesake and direct descendent of the first child born to the Pilgrims at Cape Cod Harbor in 1620.

Of his early training nothing has been discovered, although it is inferred that he may have been apprenticed in Massachusetts. In 1774 he bought a shop a little west of Muddy Brook Village equipped with "all manner of tools and implements for working in metal." He was a silversmith and clockmaker who carried on the business for many years and produced a number of excellent brass clocks, some of them with engraved dials, and others, of later date, with the ordinary white enameled dials. He was also a maker of surveyors' compasses and other small brass goods.

On March 1, 1787, he married Rebecca Bacon of Woodstock. He was a member of the Universalist Church of Oxford in 1786, and late in life a member of the Putnam Lodge of Masons. He died at Woodstock in 1834, age eighty-seven years.

JOHN WHITEAR, *Fairfield*

(B. —D. 1762)

John Whitear appears in Fairfield records in 1736, when he was a member of the Church of England under the pastorship of Rev. Henry Caner. On May 29, 1738, he advertised in the *Boston Gazette:*

> John Whitear of Fairfield (Conn.) Bell-Founder, makes and sells all sorts of Bells from the lowest size to Two-Thousand Weight.

About the year 1744 he cast the bell presented to Christ Church,

Stratford, by Dr. Johnson, Rector of that church. A clock was purchased for the church in 1750, and it is not unlikely that it was also made by Whitear.

He had at least four children born in Fairfield. He was a warden of Trinity Church in 1761, and died intestate in 1762, his estate being settled by his son John. He was an early and successful bell founder and clockmaker, and was succeeded in both branches of the business by his son.

JOHN WHITEAR, JR., *Fairfield*
(B. 1738—D. 1773)

John Whitear, Jr., was born in Fairfield in 1738, a son of John Whitear, the bell founder. He was a member of Trinity (Episcopal) Church of Fairfield, and resided in the neighborhood known as Black Rock. He undoubtedly served an apprenticeship under his father, and following the death of the latter in 1762, he succeeded to the business. In 1767 he was appointed an Ensign of the second trainband of Fairfield, and in 1771 was promoted to Lieutenant. On June 11, 1767, he married Abigail Rowland (b. 1742—d. 1813), a member of Christ Church, Fairfield. In 1762 he made an eight-day brass clock for Peter Perry and a few years later cast large bells for Colchester, Cheshire and Farmington. Early in 1769 he made his will, being at that time "weak in body;" but he recovered from that illness. He died August 26, 1773, in his 35th year and was buried in the old Fairfield burying ground where his tombstone still stands. He left no children, which was perhaps fortunate, as his estate was insolvent. His shop equipment was, however, very extensive, as appears from the following inventory prepared in November 1773 by David Burr, Jr., and William Levesay.

1 WATCH	3–0–0	1 SCREW PLATE	3–0
1 SCREW PLATE	1–2	CROOKED STAKE	0–6
1 OLD VISE	4–0	HORSE HEAD	0–6
1 OLD WATCH	1–10–0	1 WHET STONE	2–0

	HAND VISE	2–0
	TURNING LATHE	3–0
I	TURNING LATHE WITH A WHEEL	6–0
	ENGINE	7–0–0
	OLD VISE	8–0
	NEW VISE	10–0
	SMALL BENCH VISE	5–0
2	SMALL TURN KEYS	0–2
	SMALL TURNING LATHE	1–0
I	BLASTING LADLE	1–6
3	HANDLES FOR LADLES	0–4
	PARCEL OF IRON WIRE	2–2
	PARCEL OF BRASS WIRE	1–3
	A PARCEL OF OLD FILES	4–0
	POLISHING FILES	0–9
3	ARBORS	0–2
I	BORAX BOX	0–2
6	PAIR IRON CLOCK WTS.	12–0
6	TURNING TOOLS	0–6
	A QUANTITY OF BLOCK TIN	4–10–0
	A PARCEL OF FILE HANDLES	0–9
	BEAM COMPASS	0–6
	SCREW COMPASS	0–4
	SMALL SCALES & WEIGHTS	0–9
2	BLACK LEAD POTS	0–9
	PARCEL OF CRUSIVELS	1–6
	OLD ENGINE	0–6
	THE SHOP PATTERNS	2–0
16	WATCH SEALS	1–6
4	WATCH KEYS	0–4
	SMALL PLIARS	0–2
7	IRON WATCH KEYS	0–7
5	PR. CLOCK HANDS	2–6
	A PARCEL OF WATCH GLASSES	3–0
3	LB. LEAD	0–6
	A BOBIN OF PENDULUM WIRE	0–6
11	PR. WATCH HANDS	1–10
	PART OF A CLOCK	3–0
	PART OF DO	30–0
29	PR. BRASS BUCKLES	14–6
3	PR. BASS STIRRUPS	9–0
	A PARCEL OF CAT GUT	0–6
	FISH LINES	2–0
	A QUANTITY OF BRASS RINGS	5–0
4	14 INCH FILES	2–0
3	10 INCH FILES	1–0
2	8 INCH FILES	0–6
2	6 INCH FILES	0–4
	SMALL SQUARE STAKE	2–6
I	PR. PLIARS	1–6
	PR. ROUND PLIARS	0–4
	SLIDING PLIARS	0–9
	SMALL HAND VISE	1–0
2	FROSTING TOOLS	0–6
I	BURNISHER	0–4
2	SMALL HAMMERS	1–0
I	SMALL SLEDGE	1–0
	HAMMER WITH FACE BROKE	0–2
I	RAISING HAMMER	0–9
3	BROCHES	0–3
	SMALL SAW	0–9
	PR. HAND SHEARS	0–6
	WIMBLE	0–3
	BRASS COVER	0–9
2	KNIFE FILES	0–4
I	DOZ. HAND SAW FILES	2–0
2	THREE SQUARE FILES	0–6

	PARCEL OF OLD FILES	0–6
	SAL AMONAC	0–3
6	PINS & NEEDLES FOR KNITTING	1–6
	BOARAX	0–3
	RASP	0–2
	PARCEL NEW FILE HANDLES	0–9
	PATTERNS FOR CLOCK HANDS	0–2
	TAPBORER	0–4
2	OLD HAMMERS	1–0
	SQUARE STAKE	3–0
	SIDE STAKE	1–0
	A PARCEL OF SPELTER	1–6
	BOTTLE WITH SPIRITS OF TURPENTINE	0–6
	PUMICE STONE	0–6
4	SHIVES	0–4
	TURNING WHEEL	3–0
6	IRON BELL SWEEPS	3–0
	SHEET IRON	4–6
	ANVIL	2–6
	PR. LARGE SHEARS	0–6
	BOTTOM STAKE	2–0
	BELL PATTERN	0–6
2	TROWELS	0–3
	HAMMER	0–8
2	GIMBLETS	0–4
	OLD HAMMER	0–6
	LARGE STEELYARD	20–0
	OLD IRON	5–6
	FORGE TONGS	0–6
	OLD BRASS	3–15–0
	BRASS OVEN LID	1–6
	LARGE BELLOWS	10–0
	BRASS CASTING LADLE	0–9
2	CLOCK FACES	30–0
	HALF YE BELL HOUSE	4–0–0

MOSES WING, *Windsor*
(B. 1760—D. 1809)

Moses Wing, a son of Samuel and Hannah Wing of Windsor, was born April 25, 1760. He served in the Revolutionary War and was present at the retreat from New York. In 1781 he married Hannah Denslow and at about the same time built a house and shop in Windsor. He was known as a goldsmith, but made brass clocks, silver spoons, knee- and shoe-buckles. Several of his clocks are running in the vicinity of Windsor. He died in 1809 and was buried in the cemetery in Windsor where his tombstone is still standing.

BENJAMIN YOUNGS, *Windsor & New York State*
(B. 1736—D. 1818)

Benjamin Youngs, the eldest son of Seth and Hannah (Lawrence) Youngs, was born in Hartford on September 23, 1736, was doubtless apprenticed to his father, and at the time of the latter's death in 1761 was working as a clockmaker and silversmith in Windsor. About 1766 he removed to Schenectady, New York, and in 1767 was a member of Capt. Nicholas Groot's company of militia. Many years later he removed to Watervliet, New York, joined the Shakers, and died in Watervliet in 1818. He carried on both clockmaking and work in silver, and a number of his tall clocks are still to be found in the vicinity of Watervliet. His account book is said to be in existence.

EBENEZER YOUNGS, *Hebron*

(B 1756—D.)

Ebenezer Youngs was born in Hebron on March 15, 1756, a son of Ebenezer and Eunice Youngs. It is possible that he was apprenticed to David Ellsworth of Windsor, for he was in Windsor in 1776 and became the father of Sarah Allyn's illegitimate son born the following year. In 1778 and 1780 he was living in Hebron and advertising as a clockmaker and goldsmith. His advertisement in the *Connecticut Gazette* of June 9, 1780 read:

> Wanted, by the Subscriber, a Journeyman Goldsmith, and an apprentice Boy about 14 or 15 years of Age to said Business. Clocks and Watches made and repaired by Ebenezer Youngs.
> Hebron, May 27, 1780.

SETH YOUNGS, *Hartford & Windsor*

(B 1711—D. 1761)

Seth Youngs was born at Southold, Long Island, on February 20, 1711, a son of Benjamin and Mercy (Landon) Youngs. It is probable that he was apprenticed to Ebenezer Parmele in Guilford. On March 19, 1734, he married Hannah Lawrence, and late in the year 1735, when twenty-fours years old, he moved to Hartford. In 1739 he made an elaborate hour glass in a pretentious case for the pulpit of the new meeting house which was completed in December of that year. His bill for the work was six pounds, but this was considered excessive and the account was compromised by the church paying £5-10-0. At about the same time he made the gilded brass weather cock and ball which surmounted the steeple, charging £53-13-6 for this work.

He was apparently of a somewhat unorthodox turn of mind and was too outspoken in his opinions to suit the temper of the town fathers, for under date of August 20, 1742, Daniel Wadsworth, the pastor of the church, noted in his diary: "Seth Youngs sentenced to be bound to his good behavior for exhorting contrary to Law, but refusing to give bond was in ye evening committed to Goal." Three days later the worthy pastor recorded that "an ugly squabble happened last night at ye goal," perhaps a further result of Seth's "exhorting."

He was not long detained in the "goal," but upon his release he left Hartford (whether by request or choice is unknown) and in the autumn of 1742 removed to Windsor, remaining in that town until 1760, then moving to Torrington, where he bought a homestead and died on July 6, 1761, age fifty years. His wife died a few months later leaving a large family of children.

While in Windsor, Seth carried on his trade and seems to have acquired some standing in the community. In 1749 he was one of a group of prominent public-spirited men who, at their own expense, built a free bridge across Tunxis Creek. In his will, executed on June 22, 1761, he left "to my three oldest sons Joseph and Benjamin and Seth all my working tools and utensils for carrying on my trade." He was undoubtedly the first clockmaker in the vicinity of Hartford, and it is considered probable that he trained Benjamin Cheney in the trade.

1

SEVENTEENTH CENTURY LANTERN CLOCK
OWNED BY THE WADSWORTH ATHENIUM

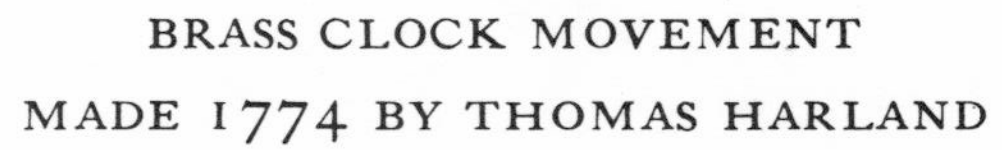

2

BRASS CLOCK MOVEMENT
MADE 1774 BY THOMAS HARLAND

3

MUSICAL CLOCK MOVEMENT

MADE C. 1785 BY DANIEL BURNAP

6

WOODEN CLOCK MOVEMENT

MADE C. 1760 BY TIMOTHY CHENEY

4
CLOCKMAKER'S LATHE
USED IN CONNECTICUT C. 1780

5
CLOCKMAKER'S ENGINE
USED IN CONNECTICUT C. 1780

7

WOODEN CLOCK MOVEMENT

MADE C. 1800 BY GIDEON ROBERTS

8

TOWER CLOCK MOVEMENT

MADE 1728 BY EBENEZER PARMELE

(IN THE STATE HISTORICAL MUSEUM, GUILFORD)

9

BENJAMIN CHENEY, EAST HARTFORD

MADE C. 1750

OWNED BY THE MC COOK FAMILY, HARTFORD

10

SETH YOUNGS, WINDSOR

MADE C. 1750

OWNED BY HENRY W. ERVING, HARTFORD

II

ISAAC DOOLITTLE, NEW HAVEN

MADE C. 1760

OWNED BY THE MISSES NEWTON, NEW HAVEN

12

RICHARDSON MINOR, STRATFORD

MADE C. 1760

OWNED BY JOHN WILCOXSON, STRATFORD

13
JOHN WHITEAR, FAIRFIELD
MADE 1762
OWNED BY F. BURR PERRY, FAIRFIELD

14

DAVID LOWREY, NEWINGTON

MADE C. 1765

OWNED BY STANLEY R. EDDY, NEW BRITAIN

15

SAMUEL ROCKWELL, MIDDLETOWN

MADE C. 1765

OWNED BY THE WADSWORTH ATHENEUM, HARTFORD

16

JOHN AVERY, PRESTON

MADE C. 1770

OWNED BY MORGAN B. BRAINARD, HARTFORD

17

NATHAN HOWELL, NEW HAVEN

MADE C. 1770

OWNED BY THE NEW HAVEN COLONY HISTORICAL SOCIETY

18

THOMAS HARLAND, NORWICH

MADE 1774

OWNED BY THE WADSWORTH ATHENEUM, HARTFORD

19

SILAS MERRIMAN, NEW HAVEN

MADE 1774

OWNED BY MRS. E. C. TERRY, HARTFORD

20

JOSEPH BULKLEY, FAIRFIELD

MADE C. 1780

OWNED BY JOHN L. CHRISTIE, FAIRFIELD

21

ASAHEL CHENEY, EAST HARTFORD

MADE C. 1783

THE MABEL BRADY GARVIN COLLECTION, YALE UNIVERSITY

22

NATHANIEL SHIPMAN, NORWICH

MADE C. 1790

OWNED BY ARTHUR L. SHIPMAN, HARTFORD

23

THOMAS HARLAND, NORWICH

MADE C. 1790

OWNED BY MORGAN B. BRAINARD, HARTFORD

24

DANIEL GRISWOLD, EAST HARTFORD

MADE C. 1790

OWNED BY GILBERT M. GRISWOLD, HARTFORD

25

PEREGRINE WHITE, WOODSTOCK

MADE C. 1790

OWNED BY WILLIAM H. PUTNAM, HARTFORD

26

ASA SIBLEY, WOODSTOCK

MADE C. 1790

OWNED BY WILLIAM H. PUTNAM, HARTFORD

27

ELI TERRY, EAST WINDSOR

MADE C. 1793

THE MABEL BRADY GARVIN COLLECTION, YALE UNIVERSITY

28

DANIEL BURNAP, EAST WINDSOR

MADE C. 1795

OWNED BY WILLIAM H. PUTNAM, HARTFORD

29

MOSES WING, WINDSOR

MADE C. 1795

OWNED BY HARRY M. HIGLEY, GLASTONBURY

30

SIMEON JOCELIN, NEW HAVEN

MADE C. 1795

OWNED BY BURTON MANSFIELD, NEW HAVEN

31

ELISHA CHENEY, MIDDLETOWN

MADE C. 1795

OWNED BY WILLIAM H. PUTNAM, HARTFORD

32

GIDEON ROBERTS, BRISTOL

MADE C. 1800

OWNED BY THOMAS W. HOOKER, HARTFORD

33

SETH YOUNGS, WINDSOR

MADE C. 1750

WNED BY HENRY W. ERVING,

HARTFORD

34

BENJAMIN CHENEY, EAST HARTFORD

MADE C. 1750

OWNED BY THE MC COOK FAMILY,

HARTFORD

35

TIMOTHY CHENEY

MADE C. 1755

OWNED BY MISS SARA HUNTINGTON, HARTFORD

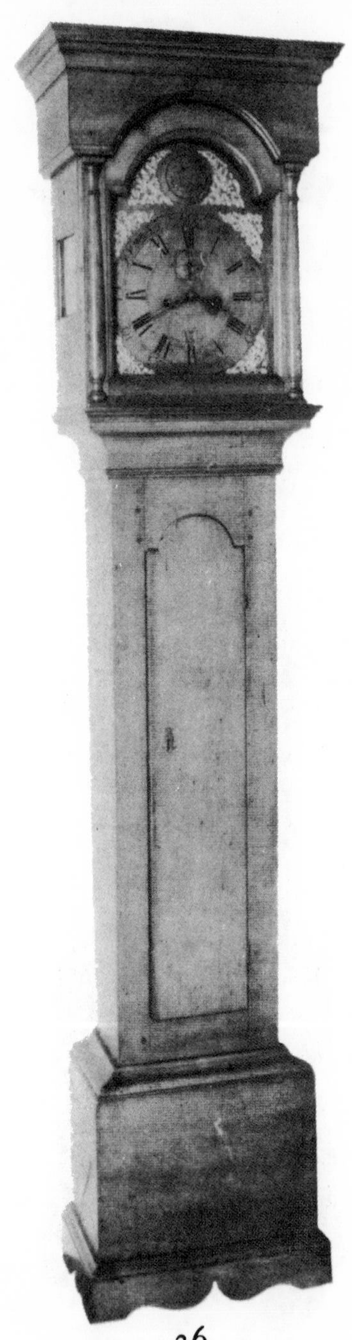

36

RICHARDSON MINOR, STRATFOR

MADE C. 1760

OWNED BY JOHN WILCOXSON

STRATFORD

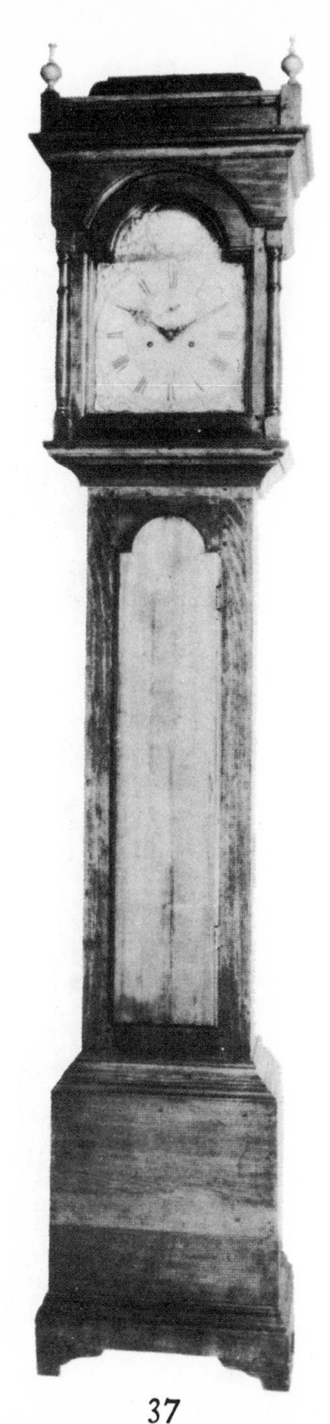

37

ISAAC DOOLITTLE, NEW HAVEN

MADE C. 1760

OWNED BY THE MISSES NEWTON, NEW HAVEN

38

JOHN WHITEAR, FAIRFIELD

MADE 1762

OWNED BY F. BURR PERRY, FAIRFIELD

39

SAMUEL ROCKWELL, MIDDLETOWN

MADE C. 1765

OWNED BY THE WADSWORTH

ATHENEUM, HARTFORD

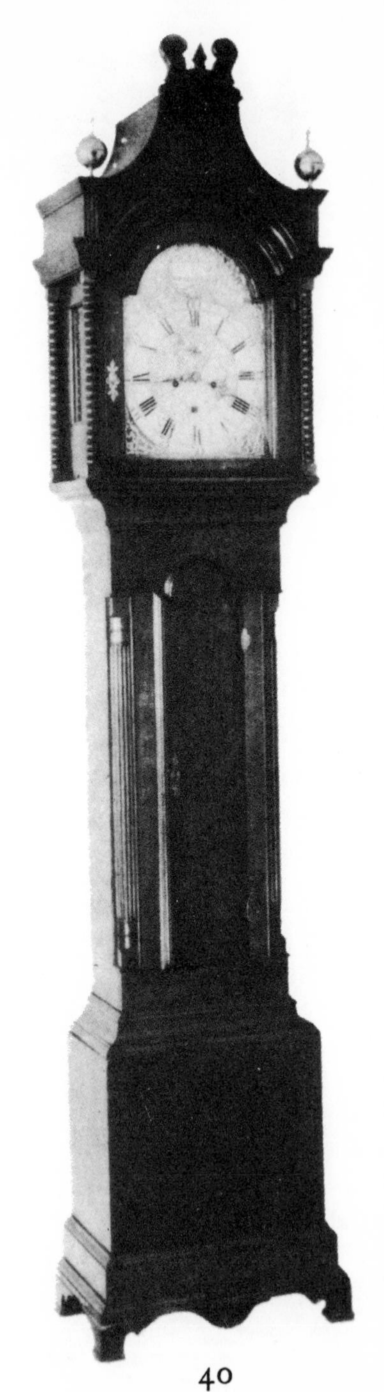

40

DAVID LOWREY, NEWINGTON

MADE C. 1765

OWNED BY STANLEY R. EDDY

NEW BRITAIN

41

NATHAN HOWELL, NEW HAVEN

MADE C. 1770

OWNED BY THE NEW HAVEN

COLONY HISTORICAL SOCIETY

42

JOHN AVERY, PRESTON

MADE C. 1770

OWNED BY MORGAN B. BRAINARD,

HARTFORD

43

SILAS MERRIMAN, NEW HAVEN

MADE 1774

OWNED BY MRS. E. C. TERRY,

HARTFORD

44

THOMAS HARLAND, NORWICH

MADE 1774

OWNED BY THE WADSWORTH

ATHENIUM, HARTFORD

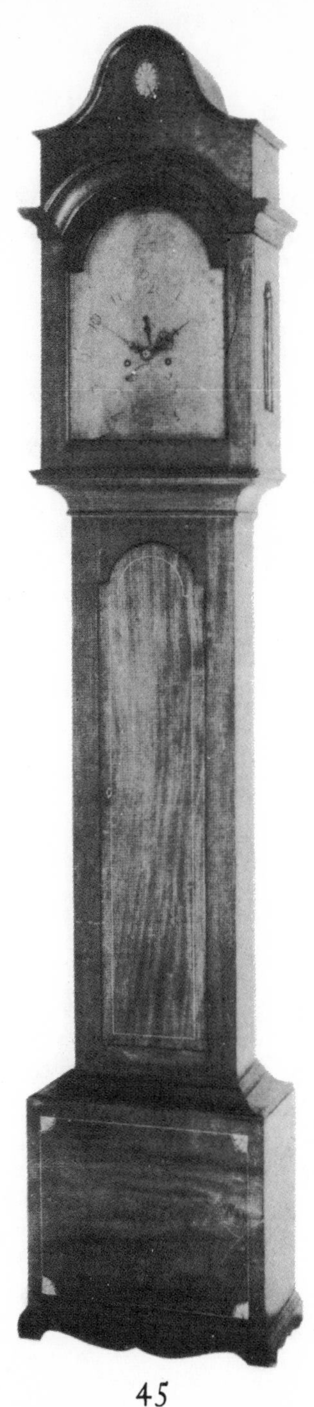

45

JOHN BENJAMIN, STRATFORD

MADE C. 1775

OWNED BY MISS FRANCES B. RUSSELL, STRATFORD

46

JOSEPH BULKLEY, FAIRFIELD

MADE 1779

OWNED BY MRS. WALTER S. WILMOT, STEPNEY

47

ASAHEL CHENEY, EAST HARTFORD

MADE C. 1783

THE MABEL BRADY GARVIN COLLECTION, YALE UNIVERSITY

48

NATHANIEL SHIPMAN, NORWICH

MADE C. 1790

OWNED BY ARTHUR L. SHIPMAN, HARTFORD

49

PEREGRINE WHITE, WOODSTOCK

MADE C. 1790

OWNED BY WILLIAM H. PUTNAM, HARTFORD

50

ASA SIBLEY, WOODSTOCK

MADE C. 1790

OWNED BY WILLIAM H. PUTNAM, HARTFORD

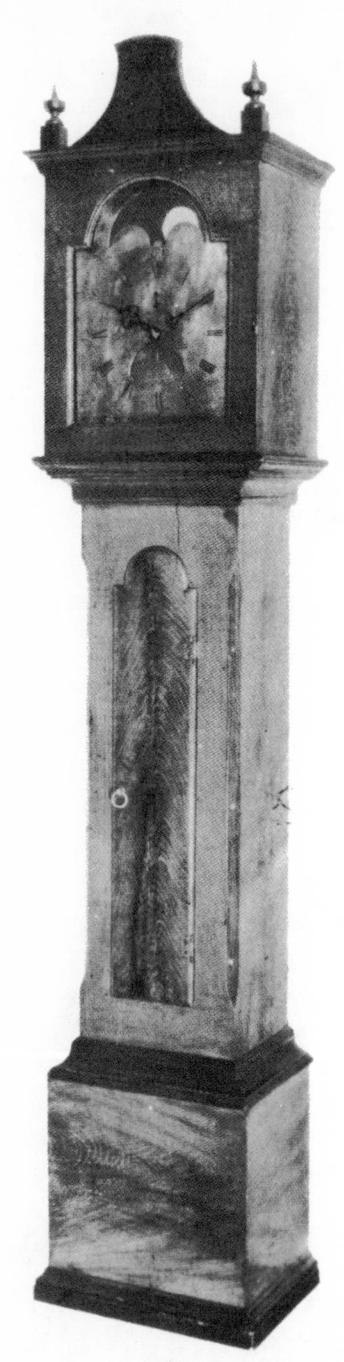

51

DANIEL GRISWOLD, EAST HARTFORD

MADE C. 1790

OWNED BY GILBERT M. GRISWOLD, HARTFORD

52

ELI TERRY, EAST WINDSOR

MADE C. 1793

THE MABEL BRADY GARVIN COLLECTION, YALE UNIVERSITY

53

ELI TERRY, EAST WINDSOR

MADE 1793

OWNED BY CHARLES I. ALLEN,

TERRYVILLE

54

DANIEL BURNAP, EAST WINDSOR

MADE C. 1795

OWNED BY WILLIAM H. PUTNAM,

HARTFORD

55

LEWIS CURTIS, FARMINGTON

MADE C. 1795

OWNED BY GEORGE CARTER,

NEW HARTFORD

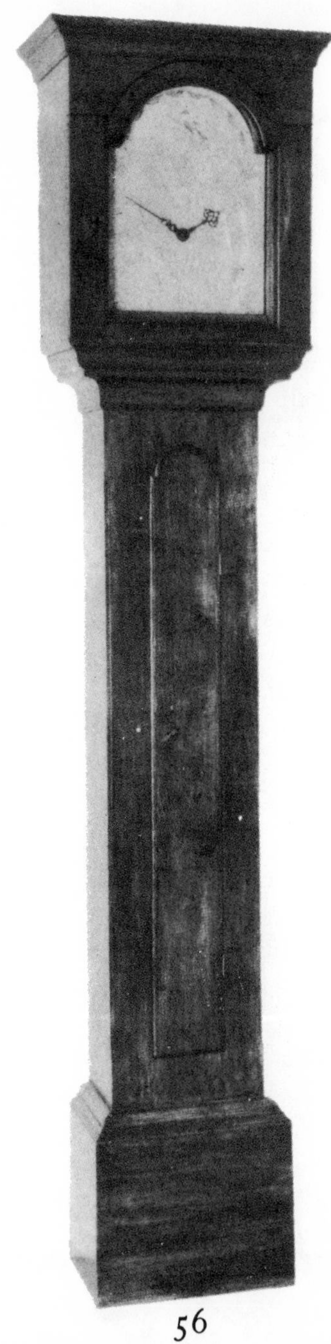

56

GIDEON ROBERTS, BRISTOL

MADE C. 1800

OWNED BY THOMAS W. HOOKER,

HARTFORD

BIBLIOGRAPHY

The Artificial Clockmaker. William Derham. London (1734).
The Elements of Clock and Watch Work. Alexander Cumming. London (1766).
English Domestic Clocks. H. Cescinski & M. Webster. London (1913).
An Introduction to the Mechanical Part of Clock and Watch Work. Thomas Hatton. London (1773).
Transactions of the Royal Society. London (1786).
United States Patent Office Records.
A History of American Manufactures. J. L. Bishop. New York (1868).
A History of Mechanical Inventions. A. P. Usher. New York (1929).
History of the American Clock Business. C. Jerome. New Haven (1860).
American Clock Making. H. Terry. Waterbury (1872).
Lists of Clockmakers.
- Old Clocks and Watches and Their Makers. F. J. Britten (1911).
- The Old Clock Book. N. H. Moore (1911).
- Early Silver of Connecticut and Its Makers. G. M. Curtis (1913).
- Early Connecticut Artists and Craftsmen. F. F. Sherman (1925).
- The Clock Book. W. Nutting (1924).

John Fitch Manuscripts. (Library Company of Philadelphia).
Account Book of Daniel Burnap.
Boston Town Records.
New England Historical & Genealogical Register.
The Arts & Crafts in New England 1704–1775, Gleanings from Boston Newspapers. G. F. Dow (1927).
The Arts & Crafts in Philadelphia, etc., 1721–1785, Gleanings from Newspapers. A. C. Prime (1929).
Diary of Rev. Daniel Wadsworth, 1737–1747.

The Literary Diary of Ezra Stiles. New York (1901).
Published Genealogies of the Families—Avery, Balch, Brewster, Carpenter, Cheney, Cleveland, Doolittle, Foot, Greenleaf, Harrison, Huntington, Merriman, Mygatt, Pitkin, Post, Reed, Shoemaker, Terry, Ward, White, Youngs.
Families of Ancient New Haven. D. L. Jacobus (Periodical).
Connecticut Archives. (Conn. State Library).
Colonial Records of Connecticut.
Connecticut Vital Records, Barbour Collection. (Conn. State Library).
Connecticut Probate Records. (Conn. State Library).
Connecticut Town Records in custody of local officials.
Connecticut Church Records in custody of local officials.
Transcripts of Town & Church Records. (Conn. State Library).
Transcripts of Town & Church Records. (Conn. Historical Society).
Connecticut Historical Society Collections.
Connecticut Newspapers.
(Danbury) Farmers Chronicle. 1793–1796.
(Danbury) Farmers Journal. 1790–1793.
(Danbury) Republican Journal. 1796–1800.
Fairfield Gazette. 1786–1789.
(Hartford) American Mercury. 1784–1800.
(Hartford) Connecticut Courant. 1764–1800.
(Hartford) Freeman's Chronicle. 1783–1784.
Hartford Gazette. 1794–1795.
Litchfield Monitor. 1784–1800.
(Middletown) Middlesex Gazette. 1785–1800.
New Haven Chronicle. 1786–1787.
(New Haven) Connecticut Gazette. 1755–1768.
(New Haven) Connecticut Journal. 1767–1800.
(New Haven) Federal Gazetteer. 1796–1797.
New Haven Gazette. 1784–1786.
New Haven Gazette. 1791.
New Haven Gazette & Connecticut Magazine. 1786–1789.
(New London) Bee. 1797–1800.
New London Gazette. 1763–1800.
New London Summary. 1758–1763.
(New London) Weekly Oracle. 1796–1800.
(Newfield) American Telegraphe. 1795–1800.

(Norwich) Courier. 1796–1800.
Norwich Packet. 1773–1800.
(Norwich) Weekly Register. 1791–1796.
(Stonington) Journal of the Times. 1798–1799.
(Suffield) Impartial Herald. 1797–1799.
Windham Herald. 1791–1800.
History of Berlin Connecticut. C. M. North (1916).
History of Danbury Connecticut. J. M. Bailey (1896).
The History of Fairfield. E. H. Schenk (1905).
The Old Burying Ground of Fairfield Connecticut. K. E. Perry (1882).
A History of the Plantation of Menunkatuck. B. C. Steiner (1897).
Colonial History of Hartford. W. D. Love (1914).
History of the First Church in Hartford. G. L. Walker (1884).
History of the Parish of Christ Church, Hartford. G. W. Russell (1895).
History of Litchfield, Connecticut. A. C. White (1920).
Residents in Litchfield, Conn., 1720–1800. G. C. Woodruff (1900).
History of Connecticut. G. H. Hollister (1855).
History of the Colony of New Haven. E. R. Lambert (1838).
History of Manchester, Connecticut. M. Spiess & P. W. Bidwell (1924).
History of Guilford, Connecticut. R. D. Smith (1877).
History of the Colony of New Haven. E. E. Atwater (1902).
History of New London, Connecticut. F. M. Caulkins (1852).
Newtown's History. J. E. Johnson (1917).
Old Houses of The Antient Town of Norwich. M. E. Perkins (1895).
History of Norwich. F. M. Caulkins (1866).
History of Plymouth, Connecticut. F. Atwater (1895).
History of Stratford and Bridgeport. S. Orcutt (1886).
History of Wallingford, Connecticut. C. E. S. Davis (1870).
The History of Waterbury, Connecticut. H. Bronson (1858).
The Town and City of Waterbury, Connecticut. J. Anderson (1896).
History of Windham County, Connecticut. E. D. Larned (1874).
The History of Woodstock, Connecticut. C. W. Bowen (1926).
History of Ancient Wethersfield, Connecticut. H. R. Stiles (1904).
History of Ancient Windsor, Connecticut. H. R. Stiles (1891).
A Modern History of New London County, Connecticut. B. T. Marshall (1922).

APPENDIX

SOME MINOR CONNECTICUT CLOCKMAKERS*

IN 1930 I published (in book form) a somewhat extensive study entitled *Connecticut Clockmakers of the Eighteenth Century.* In that volume some seventy-nine clockmakers who had been active in Connecticut prior to the year 1800 are identified and discussed in greater or less detail. During the past four years the names of several additional eighteenth-century Connecticut clockmakers have come to light, and while none of these men is of outstanding importance, nevertheless all deserve recognition as members of a trade which, perhaps more than any other, helped to prepare the groundwork for the mechanical technology characteristic of American life today. Each of these craftsmen is still represented by one or more surviving clocks.

SAMUEL CANFIELD, *Middletown*

Samuel Canfield was living in Middletown and working as a silversmith at least as early as 1780. In 1787 he was serving as sheriff. By 1790 he was, apparently, doing an extensive business in clocks, if one may judge by the amount of work done for him by Joel Allen, the engraver, whose account books are still in existence. Canfield was in partnership with William Foote in 1795-1796, and associated at various times with Noble Spencer and Elijah Yeomans, clockmakers, and with Joseph Kirkland, a watchmaker. In 1799 he threatened to sue all those indebted to him and announced that "an indiscriminate collection will take place." In 1800 he left Middletown and moved to Lansingburg, New York. It is uncertain whether Canfield himself worked at the bench as a clockmaker, or instead employed journey-

*Reproduced by courtesy of *The Magazine ANTIQUES.*

men to do the actual work. At least one clock bearing his name is still in use. Hence we must include him in our clockmakers' list.

REUBEN INGRAHAM, *Preston and Plainfield*

Reuben Ingraham was baptized July 29, 1743, at Saybrook, Connecticut, a son of John Ingraham, Jr. It is probable that his parents were of Preston, for the record of Reuben's baptism appears in the Preston church records. He became a clockmaker, perhaps under the instruction of John Avery of Preston. One of his clocks marked *R. Ingraham, Preston* is in the Garvan collection. He was living in Plainfield in 1790, when his name was recorded in the census of that year. One of his clocks with an engraved brass dial and the place name *Plainfield* has been found. Plainfield vital records note the death of "Mr. Ingraham, June 14, 1811."

THOMAS LYMAN, *Windsor*

Thomas Lyman was born at Columbia, Connecticut, January 12, 1770, a son of Deacon Thomas and Anna (Manly) Lyman. In 1781 his sister Lois married Uriah Burnap of Coventry, brother of Daniel Burnap, the noted clockmaker of East Windsor, and it is probable that, about 1785, young Lyman began an apprenticeship under Burnap. One clock is known carrying Lyman's name and the place name *Windsor*. It is fitted with a typical Burnap engraved dial. Apparently Lyman remained in Windsor but a short time after completing his apprenticeship, for his name does not appear in the Windsor records, and the genealogist of the family states that he soon removed to Ohio with his brother Jeremiah. (Mrs. Rhea Mansfield Knittle, who has made an exhaustive study of Ohio craftsmen of early days, writes that she has no record of Thomas Lyman in her list. The Western Reserve was not open until 1796, and, while Lyman could, of course, have settled in Marietta, Ohio, about 1790, no evidence to sustain that conjecture has as yet been found.)

ISAAC MARQUAND, *Fairfield*

Isaac Marquand, son of Henry Marquand and his wife Lucretia Jennings, was born in Fairfield, March 10, 1766. Henry Marquand

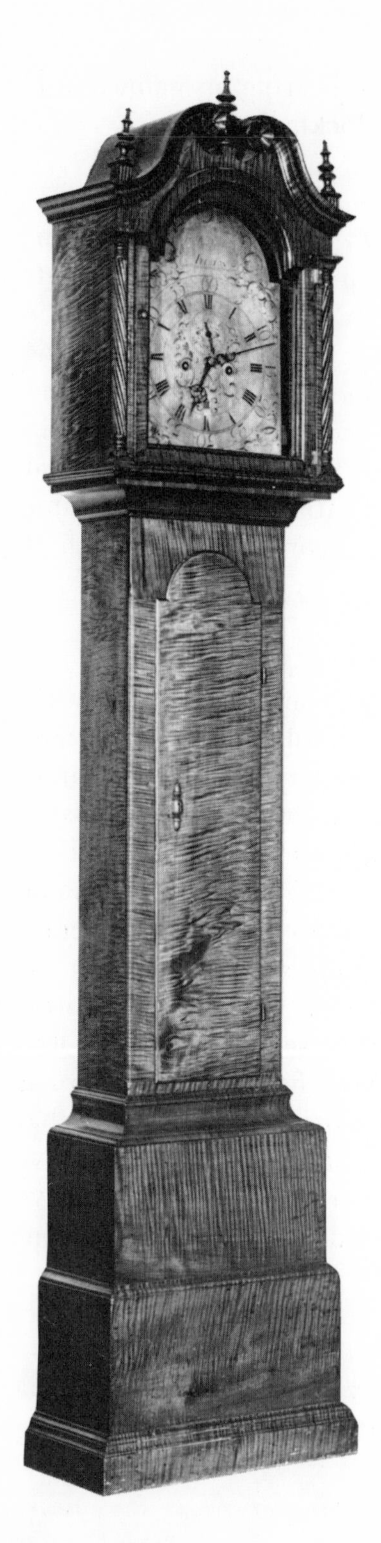

FIG. 1.

FIG. 2.

FIG. 3.

FIG. 1. CLOCK BY REUBEN INGRAHAM
Engraved brass dial inscribed *R. Ingraham, Preston.* The case is of exceptionally handsome and carefully selected maple. Ingraham also lived and worked in Plainfield. One of his clocks bearing the name of that village inscribed on the dial has been located. *By courtesy of the Mabel Brady Garvan Collection, Gallery of Fine Arts, Yale University*

FIG. 2. CLOCK BY PHINEAS NORTH
Engraved brass dial inscribed *Phineas North.* Since North claimed many accomplishments, he may quite probably have engraved the dial for this clock. The case shows peculiarities of design that suggest the possibility of North's workmanship. Detail of dial is shown in FIG. 3. *From the collection of Miss Mary Latimer*

was a joiner who had come to Fairfield from the Isle of Guernsey in 1761, and who died in 1772, leaving his joiner's tools and books on architecture to his little son. Isaac was apprenticed to his uncle Jacob Jennings, a silversmith, and, about 1787, was carrying on his own business in Fairfield. He apparently formed a partnership with one B. Whiting, for at least two clocks are known bearing the firm name *Whiting & Marquand*. Shortly after 1801 Isaac removed to New York and became a manufacturing jeweler and merchant. He died in Brooklyn, November 24, 1838.

PHINEAS NORTH, *Torrington*

Phineas North, a son of Ashbel and Ruth (Lyman) North, was born at Torrington, July 19, 1762. In 1780 he served in the Revolutionary War as a member of the 17th regiment of Connecticut militia. In 1787 he married Chloe Skinner, and in 1790 was made a freeman of Connecticut. He was a farmer, blacksmith, silversmith, and maker of brass clocks. One of his clocks carries the date *1794* engraved on the dial. He died in Torrington in 1810, leaving an extensive equipment of tools for clockmaking and silversmithing.

ANTIPAS WOODWARD, *Middletown*

Antipas Woodward was born in Waterbury in 1763, and began business as a clockmaker and silversmith in Middletown in May of 1791. On Sunday morning, January 29, 1792, a fire destroyed his shop as well as the printing office of the *Middlesex Gazette,* causing the suspension of that paper for a month. Upon its resumption Woodward advertised, March 3, 1792:

> Antipas Woodward, Respectfully informs the Public, that by the benevolence of kind Friends, he is enabled to commence Business again at the Shop lately occupied by Maj. Jonathan Otis; where any commands in his line of business will be punctually attended to. As his accounts were all consumed in the late Fire, he begs the Favor of all concerned therein to call for Settlement, as Recollection is his only Monitor.

Later in the year he moved his shop to the "Second Door North of the Coffee House" in Middletown and advertised as a goldsmith who also did clock and watch repairing. He subsequently removed to

Bristol, where, in his later years, he specialized in making wire pendulum rods for the wooden clocks turned out by Gideon Roberts and other early Bristol clockmakers. He died in Bristol in 1812.

ELIJAH YEOMANS, *Middletown*

Elijah Yeomans was the leading clockmaker of Hadley, Massachusetts, prior to the Revolutionary War. In 1777 he advertised in the Hartford *Courant*:

> Stolen from Elijah Yeomans, of Hadley, a quantity of Silver in bullien, some cash, and several other articles; the thief is one John Marris, a clockmaker, and is well known in Hartford, Middletown and Norwich. — Whoever will take up said thief, and secure him in gaol and send me word, shall have four dollars reward and necessary charges paid, by Elijah Yeomans.

In 1792 he was living in Middletown, where he advertised:

> Elijah Yeomans Watch & Clock-Maker, at Mr. Samuel Canfield's Shop, cleans and repairs Watches and Clocks, in a faithful and durable manner. Those persons who please to favor him with their Custom, may depend on having their work done with dispatch, and at reasonable prices. N.B. Miniatures neatly set.

Shortly after this time he removed to Hartford, where he worked at the shop of David Greenleaf. He died in 1794 at Hartford. A number of clocks which he made in Hadley are known, but as yet none of his Connecticut work has been found.

NAMED BUT UNKNOWN

Supplementing the foregoing additions to the list of identified early Connecticut clockmakers, the names of B. Whiting of Fairfield, Jared Brace of Newtown, and Thomas Jackson of Preston (and Boston) have been noted on one or more examples of tall clocks apparently of eighteenth-century vintage. John Marris is mentioned in Elijah Yeomans' advertisement as a well-known clockmaker in Connecticut in 1777. Just what place these men occupied in their trade I have as yet been unable to discover.

INDICES

INDEX OF NAMES

INDEX OF PLATES